InSignificant is the story of a man who has been stretched by the extent of God's love for "the least of these." Whether you are in the middle of a similar journey, looking back on the journey, or preparing to take a step of faith, this book is for you.

—Dave Stone
Senior Pastor, Southeast Christian Church

Through his experience as a teacher in a very rough school, Chris Travis has done a tremendous job of answering the question "Do I matter?" to kids who have every reason to think that the answer is no. Sometimes we just need someone like Chris to remind us that God says yes!

—Dr. Tim Harlow
Senior Pastor, Parkview Christian Church

Chris Travis has written an incredibly honest book that speaks to issues all of us wrestle with but few have the courage to talk openly about. Let his words challenge you, encourage you, and provide you with a new framework to understand your significance in this life.

—Aaron Brockett
Lead Pastor, Traders Point Christian Church

I someday hope to be an author. If that day comes, I'd love to be able to say I came close to matching Chris Travis's ability to take his readers on a journey. This story will not leave you untouched. Every teacher, pastor, communicator, and parent should read this book!

—Bert Crabbe
Lead Pastor, True North Community Church

inSIGNIFICANT

WHY YOU MATTER IN THE SURPRISING WAY GOD IS CHANGING THE WORLD

CHRIS TRAVIS

BETHANY HOUSE PUBLISHERS

a division of Baker Publishing Group
Minneapolis, Minnesota

Published by Bethany House Publishers
11400 Hampshire Avenue South
Bloomington, Minnesota 55438
www.bethanyhouse.com

Bethany House Publishers is a division of
Baker Publishing Group, Grand Rapids, Michigan

Printed in the United States of America

Library of Congress Cataloging-in-Publication Data

Travis, Chris
    InSignificant : why you matter in the surprising way God is changing the
world / Chris Travis.
        p. cm.
    Includes bibliographical references (p.   )
    ISBN 978-0-7642-0996-3 (pbk. : alk. paper)
        1. Christian sociology. 2. Vocation—Christianity. 3. Meaning (Philosophy)—
Religious aspects—Christianity. 4. Self—Religious aspects—Christianity. 5.
Self-esteem—Religious aspects—Christianity. 6. Providence and government of
God—Christianity. I. Title.
    BT738.T695 2012
    248.4—dc23   2012006413

All events in this account are factual; however, the names of certain
individuals have been changed in order to protect their privacy.

Cover design by Lookout Design, Inc.

12 13 14 15 16 17 18   7 6 5 4 3 2 1

Reader, I'd like to dedicate this book to you,
because you matter.
Read on and discover why.

Contents

Contents

Acknowledgments

It isn't possible to name everyone who contributed to this book. Take, for example, my kindergarten teacher, who taught me how to hold a pencil: What effect might her instruction have had on my future desire to write? Or what about the authors of all the books I relished in childhood, whose words taught me to love words? What about the person who loaded ink in the printers of those books? Part of the point of this book is that we often miss how significant some things are.

That said, I'd like to acknowledge some of the people whose contributions were obviously significant:

Andy McGuire believed in this book before it existed, and then improved it once it did.

Amanda Hall kept the little things from distracting from the big things.

Nathan Henrion offered valuable time and attention.

Carra Carr ensured that people knew about it.

Larry and Wendy Bennett, Matt Mueller, and Nathan Winstead offered valuable feedback to early drafts, and continue to offer invaluable work to Everyday Church.

Brent Storms, Orchard Group, and our excellent partner churches and allies all regularly expressed interest and encouragement.

The fearless and wonderful men and women I worked alongside of in that school in Harlem (you know who you are) helped to write most of this book—all of it but the words.

My parents and family loved me through the tough times that inspired this book.

Lindsay, my wife, was a perfect friend. Only she knows how true it is that I wouldn't have made it without her.

Jesus Christ was and is the only reason this book matters.

About the Author

Please Don't Skip This Part

"About the Author" sections usually come at the end of a book and share tidbits like "Chris Travis is the lead pastor of Everyday Church in New York City." A typical example would also include something personal, such as "He lives with his wife in Manhattan." If the author were in the mood to be cute, it might go on to say "He lives with his wife and two ungrateful cats in Manhattan."

All of that is true. Chris Travis does live with his wife. His cats seldom express appreciation. They all live in Manhattan together. But of course all of that isn't the whole truth. There are other true things about the author that are particularly relevant to this book. Things like "Chris knows what it feels like to be a failure." And "Chris knows what it's like to have a classroom full of students throw things at him." And "Even at his best, Chris is often rebellious against God."

Even though this is longer than the typical back-of-the-book blurb, please don't skip this part. I want you to know why I've written this book before you read it. I want to tell you what happened during the two most significant years of my life. I want to share what happened during the worst year of my life, when God crushed me, pushed me to the point of cursing him, squeezed a lot of falsehood out of me, and changed how I see things. If I hadn't gone through what I did, I wouldn't truly believe what I do about significance. I wouldn't even know it to write it.

Now I know it as well as I know anything. If I breathe, these things are true. If love exists, these things are true. I hope that by hearing some of what I went through, you'll understand why this stuff matters to you, and more to the point, why *you* matter.

We need to understand why we matter as much as we need anything. We need it like we need food or air. Our souls don't growl for it the way our stomachs growl for food, or gasp for it the way our lungs gasp for air, but we hunger and gasp nonetheless in our own ways. Even the most satisfied among us regularly shush a certain longing. It rises up and takes hold, and there it is, a listless yearning for something more, and we must quiet it in order to go on with our lives in peace. Going to church, making a purchase, having fun, keeping busy—these things stuff a pacifier in its mouth, but not for long. The hungry maw named Meaninglessness silently consumes one forgettable day after another.

Is this life going anywhere?

Will anything I do matter?

Is there something more?

Dashed Against the Nightmare Reality

"Don't think all black people are like this," the police officer said. He squeezed me in a rough bear hug. I could feel his bulletproof vest underneath his starched uniform shirt. It was like being hugged by a tree. He said these words to me, I think, because he was a black man, the principal of my school was black, and almost all the students and teachers were black. He said this to me because I was the only white person around, and I was the only one with a swollen eye.

Imagine. I used to get nervous about preaching in a church. I used to actually feel anxious before standing in front of well-mannered church people who never throw things, never push you, never threaten to rape your wife. I didn't know what it was like to stand up in front of a crowd that openly hated me, gnashed their teeth at me, and said the foulest things you can think of to me. I didn't know how it would feel to see an entire class lunge out of their seats, energized by the simple, sadistic joy of watching one kid punch another. And guess who stood between that classroom of students and the two who were fighting in the hallway.

I did, but not for long. A whole classroom of eighth-graders, some of them taller than I was, burst from the room like a shaken-up soda, and I was the bottle cap. I remember clearly the image of an eighth-grader who was taller than I jumping up and down, squealing with excitement to see the fight. In the chaos, someone slammed me against the wall, and I went home with a swollen eye.

The police officers wanted me to press charges, but I couldn't be exactly sure who it was. And if there is one thing in Harlem worse than a white teacher who wants to "make a difference," it's a white teacher who's a snitch. I wiped my tears, washed my face, and went back to class.

That happened during my second week on the job, but it wasn't the first time I had cried. The first time was after my very first day. I've never been one of those men who won't or can't cry. Men must either cry, kill, or get ulcers, and I usually choose to cry. But this was something new. I'm still not sure exactly what welled up in that moment—it surprised and frightened me. I had been up since well before the sun, taken the subway to Harlem, feverishly prepared for my class, and told myself I could do this. And then they came.

Usually, even the roughest kids will give you a few days. They call that the honeymoon period, and you've got to jump all over it to assert your authority and teach rules and procedures. But these kids came in looking for a fight. It was mayhem. They were out of their seats, at the windows, screaming, chasing each other, and throwing books. I couldn't get a word in without shouting. The moment I'd get a little control, a student would enter the class from the hallway and pick a fight with someone in my room. Or they'd just throw a pencil into class as they ran by. A student pushed me out of the way in order to get out of my class, and I was just glad he left. I tried shutting and locking the door to my classroom, but the temperature was in the 90s, and it became unbearable without the breeze. I dripped sweat all day.

At around eight thirty that evening, I slumped back in my chair and watched the cursor blinking at the end of an unfinished lesson plan. Then I threw my head back and wailed like a baby. I'm not being figurative. I can't remember the last time I sobbed like that. I think it happened sometime before I started forming memories.

There's a well-documented emotional trend first-year teachers in the inner city go through. Invariably, they fall from hopefulness into despair over the first few months, and then slowly climb back out. I think I fell in the first few hours, and the crash at the bottom almost broke me. In one moment—in one terrible breakneck tumble from the dream of "making a difference"—I dashed against the nightmare of reality. That night I woke with a start at 3:00 a.m. from a terrifying dream about teaching and cried myself back to sleep. For months I got no rest. My dreams were troubled, and I'd wake up furious at the universe for denying me sanctuary, even in sleep.

The Most Dangerous Middle School in All of New York

I wasn't clueless. I was expecting it to be very difficult. I went to a rough public school myself, and I remember kids getting jumped, knife fights, and a race riot that made the news. I had worked with inner-city kids since then, too. I had tutored since I was in middle school and throughout college. Part of my training with the New York City Teaching Fellows included teaching at a summer school program at a difficult high school.

So I thought I knew what I was getting into. I had changed careers intentionally from a staff position at a church where Lindsay and I were loved and supported. But no one could have predicted my school would be the lowest performing and most dangerous middle school in all of New York City that year. Out of nearly fifteen hundred schools and 1.1 million students in the largest public school system the world has ever known, I spent my first year teaching at the middle school with the highest rate of student injuries per capita.

The "School From Hell" is the headline *New York Post* reporter Susan Edelman chose for her article about my school. She described it as "a hellhole where teachers should get combat pay—they are cursed, assaulted and sometimes groped. . . .

"Kids hoot and yammer so loudly that their ruckus drowns out the teacher," Edelman wrote. "A trash can is overturned in class and dumped. Grimy floors are littered with sunflower-seed shells, spit out by the hundreds. Books and supplies fly out the windows." Edelman went on to explain how a gang of kids robbed a student every day for a month, how a female teacher discovered a sticky condom in her purse, how a teacher was transferred out of the school when a student threatened to rape his wife.[1]

This description was not an exaggeration. Students threw things at me, screamed obscenities in my face, stole things and ran out of the room, took their shoes off, stood on top of desks, touched girls, touched boys, and systematically went from one student to the next, disrupting education. One student like that makes it nearly impossible to teach; I had several such students in each class. There were two or three every period who seemed truly unable to control themselves. Visitors routinely asked whether my classes were for special-ed students. They were not, but it certainly seemed to me that many were in need of services I was not qualified to provide.

There was virtually no support for us. There was no phone in my classroom (it had been torn out and was never replaced in spite of requests submitted in writing). When I used my cell phone, I was reprimanded for it because we were technically not permitted to use cell phones in the classroom. If I managed to get ahold of someone to help, which was seldom, they might take the student out of the room, if the student was willing to leave, and talk to them. Then they would put them back in my class a few minutes later, at which point they would start right back up. Suspensions and expulsions came only after a lengthy legal proceeding—the discipline protocol was, in my opinion, a travesty and a grave injustice to poor and minority students. Students who finally did receive discipline often barely remembered what it was for. The rest of the students certainly had no idea why a particular student simply stopped coming to school one day, weeks after the offense. And even if they did remember, none of that mattered because being suspended was a badge of honor.

I was on my own, and I knew it.

The Slow Death of My Significance

The abuse from the students was horrible, and the resulting depression was the worst pain I've ever felt. It was far worse than any physical pain I've experienced. I would rather have one of my toes smashed with a hammer than go through it again. I remember mornings when, as I fried an egg for breakfast, the dread of the day would settle on me like some malevolent spirit, its heaviness so crippling I placed my hands on the sides of the stove and quietly wept. I cried more during that first year than I have in my entire adult life, times ten.

The deepest pain, though, wasn't the abuse. It took me a long time to find the words to describe it. Eventually I realized it was the slow death of my significance. I'd left a ministry position where I was highly regarded and where I regularly felt that my work was meaningful and effective. I've always been a hard worker and tend to excel by putting in the extra effort. I was valedictorian in high school with a 4.0 GPA—that kind of person. Being really good at what I do mattered more to me than I'd realized.

At the end of my first year teaching, I received my evaluation report and discovered that I'd performed in the bottom seventh percentile of teachers. This report supposedly accounts for all the variables—my experience, what my school is like, etc. Academic experts are in the process of debunking the accuracy of these reports, but mine sent a pretty clear message. Out of every 100 teachers in my situation, 93 were more effective than I was. Trust me, I can rationalize with the best of them about why it really wasn't my fault, but it doesn't change the fact that I was completely ineffective. I was a teacher and my students did not learn. I failed.

I also rediscovered that I'm not such a good guy. I already knew that, but the words take on a textbook quality when you've been a pastor for a while and you have a lot of encouraging people around you all the time. You start to think, *Of course I'm not perfect, but I'm a decent sort of person.*

My experience teaching drew hatred out of my heart that I didn't know was there. From time to time, I would write a verse of Scripture on an index card and carry it around with me, desperately clinging to anything that might help, hoping its promise or its encouragement would give me strength. The other day I found one of those old cards in a drawer. On the front I had written Hebrews 12:11: "No discipline seems pleasant at the time, but painful. Later on, however, it produces a harvest of righteousness and peace for those who have been trained by it." Sometimes I would splash water on my face and stare in the mirror and tell the zombie looking back at me, "Peace and righteousness. It's worth it for peace and righteousness."

On the back of that card, at some point, I angrily scrawled these words: "I hate these kids."

And the whole thing was so insignificant by any earthly standard. I was a middle school math teacher in a failing school. Nobody listened to me or cared about my opinions. All day long students despised what I thought. My words were weak and they didn't matter, not at all like when I used to speak in church and people would dab their eyes or come up and thank me afterward for the encouragement. There was no power, money, or fame.

There was something better. More on that later.

It Wasn't Until Pain

I don't know what you expect from a book like this. If you are interested in poverty or education, this book has something to say about it. I don't have any big ideas or answers, but poverty and education are the setting for much of this book, so it will naturally ask some questions and make some observations that may be helpful and should at least be interesting.

If you are interested in spiritual things, in God or the Bible, this book has something to say about those, too. You'll find that in spite of all the first-person narrative, God is in fact the protagonist. You can't miss him if you look. Those who seek, find.[2] I've never experienced God working so powerfully through me as I did during my second year of teaching.

But the real focus of this book is on significance. This is a book about what matters. I'd write a thousand books to get this point across: In the surprising way God is changing the world, you matter. This book is an attempt to explain why.

It was only after the two most difficult years of my life that I began to truly understand this simple truth about how much each of us matter. I'm sure I heard most of these concepts in seminary, but it wasn't until I went through what I did that I actually learned them. It wasn't until pain pumped blood into those words and brought them to their feet to march around my soul that I began to believe them.

I'm a slow study and needed the discipline of personal experience, but I've written this book in faith that there's more than one way to learn something. I'm hoping that reading about my experiences will be enough for you to learn what I've learned. I never dreamed I might enjoy moments in my life like I did my second year of teaching, and I wouldn't trade them for any price. I really mean that. If you offered me a billion dollars in exchange for one of these moments, I would despise the sum. Moments like these make your entire life worthwhile. I want you to have moments like that, too. You may not even realize that your soul is growling for them, gasping for them, but go ahead and take a taste.

Read. Inhale.

About the Author

About the author: "Chris Travis failed. His mentor from teacher's college was embarrassed by his performance. Chris was mean to kids sometimes. A lot of kids really hated him. He worked hard, but he was found wanting. To his surprise, though, he discovered what matters, and has received a harvest of peace and righteousness he never dared wish for."

If you would like to read what a humiliated, sinful failure has to say about what really matters, then I have just the book for you. We begin with a true paradox: The two years I spent teaching math in Harlem were the two most significant years of my life. They were also the most insignificant.

First Things Last

Power Is Powerless to Change the Heart

It Broke His Heart

I'm not sure I can explain why I decided to teach at that school. Something stirred in my heart—I felt drawn to it, much the way I imagine certain people are drawn to the ocean. I knew there were dangers I didn't understand, but I had to go.

My wife and I had planned to move to New York City for a variety of reasons. Part of it was that Lindsay is an actress in musical theatre, and part of it was that we had a sense we would plant a new church there at some point. I had been working on staff at a church, so naturally my first impulse was to find a ministry position somewhere. But when I stumbled across the New York City Teaching Fellows, I knew it was what I wanted to do. There is injustice in public schools in the form of a measurable achievement gap. White and Asian students tend to out-perform black and Hispanic students. Rich students out-perform poor students. The New York City Teaching Fellows program attempts to close the achievement gap through a simple strategy: Put good teachers in bad schools.[1]

I wanted to do something significant. Meanwhile, I think God wanted to give me a tiny glimpse of what it's like to be him. Leaving the security and comfort of a good life with good friends and a good job and entering such a painful situation gave me a small picture into what God did for us. Unfortunately, I discovered I'm not much like him at all.

Imagine for a moment what it's like to be God. I know that sounds weird, but I'm not saying imagine what it would be like if you *were* God. We aren't and never will be. And trust me, we should all breathe a sigh of relief about that. Imagine what it's like for *God* to be God—the real God, the One who actually exists. Even if you are unsure what you believe, I'd like you to take a moment simply to imagine. God is remarkably vulnerable and transparent in the Bible—in fact, he's much more open about his feelings than most of us are with each other. When was the last time you admitted that someone hurt your feelings? Too old for that? God isn't.

Try to imagine being eternal. Picture those times in life you wished would never end. I remember days in the summer, lying in the grass, watching the clouds roll by. Maybe you've felt it when you finished a really good book, the sweet pang of sadness. If only you could have a little more time in that world. If only we could hang on to the joy, or thrill, or beauty for one moment longer. Those moments ache with mortality. They always end. We have to go to work, back to school, we get sick, we say good-bye . . .

But try to imagine the feeling that would answer that ache. Try to imagine having that hunger filled—the constant relief of knowing the good things would never end. This is how God felt before the beginning.

Have you ever been in love? I mean young love, the kind of love that does stupid things—writes bad poetry and talks on the phone for hours. The kind that thinks picking her up Friday at eight is way too far off. When will your shift be over so you can be together? In love, all food tastes better, all fun is funnier, all danger more thrilling. Everything that matters, matters more; and nothing else matters at all.

God the Father, the Son, and the Holy Spirit is love.[2] This is how God felt before the beginning.

Imagine what it would feel like to completely belong. Maybe you've had a friend who would do for you without asking why. Maybe you have family who act like family; blood that's thicker than water. You may remember a band of brothers from high school or college, or close girlfriends who would hate him forever if he ever did you wrong.

God the Trinity is one God, but he has never been alone. This is how God felt before the beginning.

Have you ever felt capable, confident? You knew what to say? You were in your sweet spot? This was your time to shine. This is how God felt before the beginning.

God lacks nothing. He overflows. He was so content, so satisfied, so overflowing with love that he created others to love. He created us, in his image, free to love one another and free to love him back.

Or free not to love at all.

Not long after the beginning, God felt something different. "The LORD observed the extent of human wickedness on the earth, and he saw that everything they thought or imagined was consistently and totally evil. So the LORD was sorry he had ever made them and put them on the earth. It broke his heart."[3]

It broke his heart.

It Was the Only Way to Get Through

The first time I visited the Polo Grounds, a notorious housing project in Harlem, it changed my view of American poverty. Several government towers stretched to the sky, casting long shadows over the muddy lawns. Hundreds of cinder-block apartments stared down at the playgrounds where gangs attempted to recruit kids my students' age. The promise of a little protection must be so tempting to a twelve-year-old who walks home from school every day under the fear of attack. Only later do these younger recruits have to participate—violence for boys, sex for girls.

We couldn't go near the base of the buildings because people periodically dropped trash or bottles out of the windows, sometimes from almost thirty stories above. You could lose your life that way. Inside, the buildings were cold—all the windows were busted out and the wind whipped through the exterior halls. The cinder-block walls were covered in graffiti and territorial markings.

I figured most residents would assume that a white guy in a tie was either a cop or with Child Protective Services. At night, being white might have made me a target, but during the daytime it offered a little protection. But we didn't go alone. The teachers at my school really hustled to develop positive relationships with our students' families. Several times I tagged along with more experienced teachers to make home visits. It was often the only way to get through.

I've seen poverty before—in Eastern Europe, in Southeast Asia. But there were moments in the Polo Grounds when it was difficult to believe I was in the United States. I can't imagine how a kid could grow up there with a positive view of anything. The Polo Grounds' reputation for murder had me a little on edge each time we visited. Shootings were common.

We would try to convince their families that school was important, but many of my students had lost parents to violence or overdose and shouldered responsibilities I didn't have to take on until I was an adult, like caring for siblings or finding food. Some of my students had to be home before dark and never got to go outside. They longed for the freedom to ride their bikes in the Dominican Republic or down South (where relatives lived in Georgia or Mississippi), but they were here instead because there weren't jobs or it wasn't safe or for some other reason.

We like to think the world Jesus came to save—a world in which Romans were perfecting the art of crucifixion—was much more brutal and awful than ours is. We like to think things are getting better. Some things are much better. There is better medicine and transportation and information.

Other things are worse. There are tens of thousands of warheads in the world. Despots as scary as Hitler fight to secure them. Airplanes fly into towers full of civilians. Scientists are busy trying to synthetically mutate and weaponize microorganisms so they can kill enemies better and quicker. The wheat and the weeds grow up together.[4]

I stood in the killing fields in Cambodia once and felt the gears of denial begin to turn in my mind. It was too appalling to be true. There was a monument made out of hundreds of human skulls. I overheard a guy from Canada mumbling to himself what I wished I could believe: "We would never let this happen today. We would stop it. This could never happen today."

But it is happening today, I thought. Sudan. Burma. Democratic Republic of Congo. Afghanistan. Pakistan. Iraq. Somalia.[5]

Today there are millions of slaves in the world, most used for sex or labor, all for making someone else money. There are more slaves today than there ever have been before. Many are abused savagely if they do not perform. Many are children, like Nomi.

Nomi is a little girl in Cambodia. She was eight years old when she was rescued from sexual slavery. The physical and sexual abuse was so severe that she suffers permanent mental disabilities from the trauma. I'll talk more about her in a few pages.

The Five-O'clock News Doesn't Cover the Scariest Thing

In those first months, I was reeling from the ugliness of it all. There were some really bad fights. Girls scratched each other bloody. I took a sick day and my eighth-graders trashed my room. They ripped up student work, ripped up books, wrote on the walls, pulled everything out of my desk and closets and destroyed it, stomped Wite-Out containers all over the floor, and sprayed white paint on the chalkboards.

Another class stopped up the sink in their room and flooded it. One of the deans got into a full-out fist fight with a student.

A student threw a metal pipe out the window and hit a teacher. He was arrested.

I was pretty broken—I felt useless and devastated—and I was looking for a way out. When I received a phone call from one of the principals of a school I had applied to the previous summer, I assumed the Lord had heard my prayers and was making a way out for me. I took a sick day and nailed the interview. I knew the day off would mean hours of cleanup in my classroom after school, but it felt worth it. In part of the interview I had to demonstrate a lesson. The kids I taught that day were inner-city kids, too, but the environment was very different. I had them in check and had such a great time teaching. The principal said she couldn't believe I was a first-year teacher. The seventh-grade classes actually wrote her a letter asking her to hire me. I'm not kidding.

I was feeling so useless and fragile at that point, and this experience really helped me get some perspective. But then I went back to my school, where the students hated me openly and hated themselves. And according to my contract, the only way I could leave at that point in the year was for the principal to release me. Life for me would have been so much better at this other school. It was the wise thing to do. I sought all kinds of counsel, and it really made the best sense. I asked a bunch of people to pray about it with me. I was ready to ask for the release.

Over the next few days I had three separate experiences in which I sensed God saying to me, "I want you to stay." I don't want to go into details; they aren't important. I know for some readers, talking about "hearing God" sounds weird, bordering on unstable. I tend to be rather skeptical about this sort of thing, too, as you will see. But this was one of the few times in my life when I had a very strong sense God wanted me to do something specific. He wanted me to stay. Annoyed, I decided I needed something clearer to go on than a "strong sense God wanted me to do something specific."

One night before going to sleep, I wrote the following in my journal:

> Lord, please lead me and guide me this week. Make it clear, clear, clear. I need to be released by my principal. But more important, I need to be released by you. Please give me the sense of release. If your will is that I stay, then I need something a bit stronger than gut feelings. I'm not saying you have to send an angel, but I need something more than a vague, flickering notion. I need you to hit me with it.

I had developed a friendship with two strong, godly women who taught at my school. They constantly looked out for me and helped me along. The morning after I wrote those words, one of the ladies came into my classroom as I prepared for the day. She got right to the point. "I can't believe I'm even doing this, 'cause you know how badly *I* want out of here. But the Lord told me to ask you, 'You're worried about being released by the principal, but have you been released by me?' And he told me to say to you, 'I want you to stay.'"

I was stunned speechless. When she left the room, I wept. Not because I had just had such a chilling spiritual moment, but because I already knew that was what he wanted, and I was miserable about it.

I knew what God wanted but decided to do the opposite. I went and asked my principal to release me anyway. I begged her to do it, but she refused. She said she wouldn't be able to find a replacement and so couldn't afford to let me go. Given how bad things were at the school, she was probably right.

I know you want to let me off the hook. I do, too. It was such a tough situation, who could blame me? Does God even talk to us like that?

Nonsense. I knew what he wanted, and according to the Bible, "Rebellion is as sinful as witchcraft."[6] I was lying when I had said I just wanted him to be clear about his will. I wasn't interested in his will at all. Everyone agrees with the basic moral imperatives of Scripture. We all think if the world worked the way it should, we wouldn't steal or lie or murder. I think, *Yeah, people shouldn't be selfish*. People should sacrifice and give to others. But when it comes to me sacrificing for others, I'm quick to find a way out. I consistently look out for myself and care little about what's best for everyone else.

The world is a dark place, but the five-o'clock news doesn't cover the scariest thing about it. The lying and stealing and killing isn't even the worst part. Those things are the bite, not the snake. The scariest thing is that our hearts haven't changed. When it comes down to it, I care more about myself, my wife, and my stuff than I do about yours. We care more about our own stuff, our country, our kids than we do about theirs. We can hardly imagine how it could be any other way. I put myself first. We all do.

"All of us have become like one who is unclean, and all our righteous acts are like filthy rags; we all shrivel up like a leaf, and like the wind our sins sweep us away."[7]

God help us.

Instead He Comes Wooing

That's exactly what God did. He came and helped us. He entered the world as a man named Jesus. This is where things get particularly confusing.

If God wanted to, he could appear as a great dragon, a fearsome, ruthless monstrosity—a glittering mountain of muscles writhing underneath rows of impenetrable scales. He could rip the earth from the sky like a scab and fling it aside, bare his teeth, and bellow, "I AM! I AM! I AM!"

Or he could come as a mighty king, as one of the kings we begged him for back in the days before God's people had kings. He would shatter injustice with his scepter and sweep away sin with a snarl.

Instead, he "grew up in the LORD's presence like a tender green shoot, like a root in dry ground. There was nothing beautiful or majestic about his appearance, nothing to attract us to him."[8] Instead, he came as a baby. He came into the Polo Grounds as a vulnerable baby and lived a life of love, armed only with words.

They spit on him and played games with him, clenching their fists and punching him in the face. They taunted, "Prophesy to us! Who hit you that time?"[9] They brought the hammer down hard enough to drive nails into wood. They gambled for his clothes while he hung naked. They executed him as a criminal and hung his agony on display between two guilty men.

But he never did anything wrong. Never once. He never even had the wrong motives. Hanging from the cross, he prayed for them. The perfectly righteous Son of God conquered sin, not through victory, but through defeat. Between his final breaths, wheezing for air, he prayed.

"Father, forgive them."[10]

The greatest indictment of this world in history is that we killed Jesus. We killed Love.

God put himself last. I'm not sure what we would do if we were God. Probably stupid things that would only make us and everyone else miserable. Regardless, I am certain we would not go about getting what we wanted the way God chose to. I imagine we'd use more force. We would put ourselves and our agendas first. But instead of forcing us, God persuades. It seems backward. If we saw things clearly, we'd be begging him to be in a relationship with us. Instead, he comes wooing, pursuing, serving. There is no other god who seeks like this, not in heaven or on earth, in truth or in fiction, not in our wildest dreams or imaginings. Only the God of the Bible stoops, whispers, touches gently.

If you are wondering why God is so long in destroying evil, it is for the sake of love. "The Lord isn't really being slow about his promise, as some people think. No, he is being patient for your sake. He does not want anyone to be destroyed, but wants everyone to repent."[11] Many people who shake their fist at God because he allows so much evil have no idea what they're saying. They haven't looked into their own hearts long enough to contemplate the horror of justice. That day will come, but in the meantime, God still enters the world humbly. He comes in ways we might not expect and often works through the weak, the powerless, and the ordinary.

Nomi, the girl I mentioned earlier, now lives with other girls who have been rescued from sexual exploitation in a Christ-centered rehabilitation home in Cambodia. Unlike her housemates, she will likely never leave because her traumatic experiences in sexual slavery have left her permanently mentally disabled. But she is finding hope and a renewed life. She runs, laughs, and plays with her friends. She giggles when the older girls tickle her. When she has to sit through school lessons, she sighs wearily. But she focuses her concentration when it comes to feeding the pet bunnies.[12]

One day, some women were visiting ministries in Cambodia, seeking to rescue people from slavery. At this particular home for girls, Nomi ran to them and gave them a hug. That was the moment when one of the women knew she had to join the fight against human trafficking. It was Nomi's hug that prompted her to act, and she went on to found the Nomi Network.

Human trafficking is a profit-driven problem, so Nomi Network offers a market-based solution. They support the local ministry in Cambodia using what they know: film and fashion. They work with the rescued women to design fashionable handbags and then help market them here in the States. They leverage their network to give these recovering women the dignity of a respectable profession and the potential for financial independence. As part of a holistic approach to helping them, it's brilliant. NBC announced that the Nomi Network received the Small Charity of the Year award.[13]

God is changing the world in a surprising way.

That's real power. God wields the soft and unassuming power of love. It isn't flashy and it isn't trendy, but it is the only thing that can change the human heart.

There is something very powerful about being with people. It's disarming. Many of my students seldom had the opportunity to inspect a white person up close. Some of them were fascinated with my blue eyes. "Those contacts?" they asked.

"No, these are my eyes."

"I wish I had eyes like that."

"Don't be silly. I think brown eyes are much more beautiful. My wife has brown eyes."

I remember a moment when I returned from winter break that first year. I leaned over a student's desk to help with a problem and got a strong whiff of hair product. Black hair product had been mostly alien to me, and my palate didn't understand the aroma. But something had changed in me, and it now smelled delightful. I inhaled deeply and marveled at how easily the taste was acquired. I simply had to be around it to appreciate it.

I'm not sure I can explain why I went to teach at that school. It wasn't because I was a good person. For all my talk about wanting to be more like Jesus, I didn't really want to put myself last for others as he did. But God knew what I didn't.

He knew he could change me, too.

What Does He Want From Us?

We Never Would've Guessed What God Is After

"Shantel! Shantel!" I called down the hallway after her, but she ignored me.

Every parent has this experience. As a teacher, it happened all the time. This time I was calling her because I had a bag of Starburst, and I was going to give her some. Of course, she assumed I was calling her name in order to tell her to do something she didn't want to do. If only she knew.

I suppose I could have made her obey. I could have run fast enough to catch her, and I was stronger than her. "You'll take this Starburst and you'll like it!" But that wouldn't have gotten me anywhere regarding her heart.

I can say with integrity that my rules and instructions existed to make things better for my students. I didn't make my students get permission to leave their seats just because

I liked watching kids sit. I knew if Kareem got up without permission and came anywhere near Marquel, it could escalate from a friendly jab to desks getting flipped and innocent girls getting hurt in seconds. When I said, "Please don't stick your gum there," it was in the best interest of everyone else who would use that chair. Nobody wants to see or touch other people's chewed gum.

If every kid followed all of my rules and directions unquestioningly, they would have had more fun than they imagined possible in math class, and they would have learned a ton, too.

But it was hard to trust this old guy they didn't know very well. (It was hilarious how old they thought a man in his thirties was—I used to tell them I was seventy-three, and they believed me!) It was hard for them to believe the big picture. They didn't have the vantage point I had. I could see that if they called out when they hadn't been called on, they contributed to a culture in which no one would listen to them when it was their turn. It was hard for them to believe that when the old dude asked for something, even though it might not have seemed to be in their best interest, it was.

I don't want to push this metaphor too far, and I don't want to be overly simplistic about what it means to follow Jesus. Following Jesus is definitely not rule-following. But it is not rule-ignoring, either. Jesus is doing something much more significant than imposing a set of rules on a chaotic classroom. Jesus is ushering in an entirely new kingdom. The rules aren't dos or don'ts that we get to choose whether or not to obey. They are statements about a coming reality. They are as nonnegotiable as gravity. In the kingdom of God, people forgive one another. That's just how it is. The choice isn't whether you want to forgive so-and-so. The choice is whether you want to be a part of God's kingdom or not.

The Experts Were Not Often Excited

Jesus' words have been repeated so many millions of times over thousands of years that they've taken on an almost musical quality: beautiful, but missing their teeth. His first words had a bite that we need to recapture.

When Jesus entered Jerusalem for the final time, he came bouncing in on the back of a borrowed donkey, leading a train of prostitutes, tax collectors, uneducated tradesmen, and children. I imagine his eyes twinkled when the crowds praised God: "Hosanna! Blessed is he who comes in the name of the Lord!"[1] They laid palm branches across his path, and the moment was so pivotal in history that today, two thousand years later, hundreds of millions of people wave palm branches on Palm Sunday in memory of it, all over the world, in massive cathedrals and tiny country chapels, in Iowa and in Africa.

Men like Judas must have thought, *This is it! Finally a king to rule with an iron scepter! Finally a man who will prove us right, set us free, and step on Rome's neck!*

But Jesus' zeal was for his Father's house, the temple. He entered the courts that had been designated for worshipers from all nations, but instead of the sounds of prayer in many languages, he was greeted by clanking coins on the money changers' tables and the snorting and clucking of animals for sale. Surveying such an irreverent din of profiteering, I imagine the twinkle in his eyes darkened, now smoldering with a holy fire. Calmly, he crafted a whip out of cords. Armed with it and words as sharp as razors, he overturned tables and drove from the temple both beasts and brokers. In his whole life and ministry, this was the first and only time Jesus used force to make a point. To the stunned crowd he cried, "My house will be called a house of prayer for all nations!"[2]

He began to teach, and the religious experts came forward to test him. They were masters of the Scriptures; many had them memorized. Sitting under their teaching, you or I might often have thought, *I don't think God is really like that.* But we couldn't even step into the ring with them because they could crush us with the Scriptures.

But Jesus, a carpenter from the sticks, responded like this: "You are in error because you don't know the Scriptures or the power of God."[3] To men who had the Scriptures memorized, he said, "You do not know the Scriptures." He responded to their legal traps with such decisive mastery of the text, crowds were "astonished at his teaching."[4]

One tested Jesus with this question: "Teacher, which is the greatest commandment in the Law?"[5]

Talk about an important moment in the Bible. This is Jesus Christ. He is God in the flesh, walking the world as a normal man. They asked him, of all the hundreds of laws in the Bible, which is the most important? If there's a weird situation where it seems like two different laws are at odds, which one wins? If I learned only one command, which should it be?

Amazingly, Jesus actually answered him. But he didn't answer the way we would expect a great teacher of the law might. I would have expected him to say something very spiritual-sounding, like, "All the commandments are of equal importance." Or maybe, "The law doesn't work like that. It is all to be valued, weighed, and obeyed equally." Or I might have expected him to respond with some kind of Yoda-like guru wisdom. Something deep like, "My son, you must focus on the commandment that seems the least pleasant to you."

He doesn't. He simply answers the question. Out of the hundreds of commandments in the Bible, Jesus picks one.

It Took Me About a Year

I began to believe in Jesus years before stepping into that grungy third-floor classroom. Or at least I thought I had. In reality, I had only begun the process of trusting him. Before teaching in Harlem, I would have said my relationship with God was the most important thing in my life. I did not realize how much I depended upon other things.

I had no idea how much I needed to be esteemed and spoken kindly to by the people around me. I had no idea how much respect mattered to me. I had no idea how much of my significance was tied up in being good at what I did and being recognized for it. There was no getting around the fact that I was failing. As I mentioned before, I can easily rationalize my failure. The system stunk, and some of my students' parents made it difficult for them to even want to learn. Funding was so tight our supplies were like a bad joke. But the truth remains: My classroom was out of control, and my students weren't learning. They also disliked me and had good reasons. Most days I really disliked them. I'm too embarrassed to share my worst journal entries with you. Imagine the words *hate* and *kids* mixed into a variety of expletives with lots of frantic underlining, and you'll get the idea.

In the middle of some of the worst pain, a friend of mine named Dick Alexander told me a story that flipped a switch in my soul. Dick had been a huge influence on my life for many years. When I decided to be baptized, it was in response to one of Dick's sermons. Later, when the same church hired me on staff as one of the pastors, he became my boss. Dick has been a mentor of mine, and during that first year of teaching, he and I touched base from time to time. At one point he told me about a difficult year he had when he was about my age. He had moved to do youth and children's ministry in an older church that was attempting to pull off a revival. One Sunday morning he was thinking about Bible college classmates who were off leading churches while he was doing children's ministry in the basement with twenty-three kids. A question began running through his mind: "If I spend the rest of my life doing children's ministry in the basement, will that be enough? Do I need to be 'successful'?" Dick explained to me that it took him about a year to "stare down the lion of success and decide anonymity for Jesus would be enough."

Is Jesus enough? That question wrecked me. It haunted me. What if this was God's will for the rest of my life? What if he wanted me to work at this little inner-city middle school in central Harlem, to be mostly miserable and ineffective, and to rarely ever see any reason to believe I was making a difference? Was Jesus enough for me?

It took me about a year to answer that question, too. I had no idea then that I was contemplating the most important thing in life. God was reversing all my ideas about significance and clarifying in me a simple conviction: There is one thing we can do with our lives that is so significant, everything else is insignificant. Just beginning to grasp the implications of this truth has given me a peace, hope, and passion I never expected.

God Does Not Want to Be an Important Part of Your Life

"Love the Lord your God with all your heart and with all your soul and with all your mind," Jesus replied. "This is the first and greatest commandment."[6]

Jesus said the greatest commandment is to love God.

He didn't say worship, serve, obey, or give. He didn't even say the greatest commandment was to believe. All these things are important, and they may even be a part of what it means to love. But that doesn't take away from the simple fact that Jesus said the greatest commandment was to love God.

This is the most significant thing you can do in life.

Love God with all your heart. The heart is the center of your will. It is the place where your desires are formed and where your dreams are dreamed. It is where your decisions are made. This is love from the inside out, not only doing it, but *wanting* it.

Love God with all your soul. This is more than just loving God with your actions. You cannot simply go through the motions. You cannot just say the prayers, do the rituals, go to church, and forget about it. True worshipers worship in Spirit and in truth.[7]

Love God with all your mind. Love him with all your thoughts and understanding. You mustn't harbor secret reservations and doubts, but rather seek answers and ask questions. You mustn't pretend to believe what you do not, but rather continue to learn and seek understanding. You mustn't accept things simply because someone else says to, but instead test everything, asking whether it is true.

Love the Lord your God with all you have. On the one hand, this is much simpler than we typically try to make things. It lifts a burden. Jesus said, "My yoke is easy and my burden is light."[8] Do not be crushed by all the rules. Do not let all the should-do's strangle your relationship with God. He wants your love. We get off track worrying about all sorts of other things that Jesus says are less important than loving God. This is the first thing to do before anything else.

On the other hand, this is far more challenging than we would ever dare to ask of ourselves. Three times Jesus says the word *all*. With *all* your heart, *all* your soul, and *all* your mind. God does not want us to love him with *some*. He wants us to love him with all we are and all we have.

God does not want to be an *important* part of our lives. He wants it all.

And Something Wonderful Happened

One of the most surprising things about God is what he's after. Simply put, God wants a relationship with us. He wants a relationship with you. This is one of the surprising ways in which we matter. God actually wants to know us and to be known by us.

He lacks nothing. It's not as if he has a fragile ego and needs our worship to feel important. We worship because he is that incredible. The better you get to know him, the more spontaneous worship is. And it's not as if he gets some kind of power trip or entertainment value out of watching us scurrying around to serve him. There is nothing we can offer the God who created us out of nothing, except the one thing he gave us power over: our love. God wants a hold-nothing-back love relationship with us. He gave himself completely for us and wants us to give ourselves completely to him.

Is God enough for you?

If he never answers another prayer? If you never get married? If your husband never comes back? If this is the best job you'll ever have? If you get cancer and die? If *she* dies? If it all crashes tomorrow and you lose everything? If your dreams never come true? If it is difficult and only gets more difficult, and there's silence from heaven, is what Jesus did for you enough?

If it isn't, don't fake it. Tell him. "God, it's not enough for me. I need something else." Trust me, he knows what's in your heart, whether you have the courage to say it or not. Hiding from God hasn't worked since Adam and Eve ducked into Eden's undergrowth, so don't waste your time. Be straightforward with him. If there's anything in you that's stuck on that question, don't brush it off.

It's embarrassing how long it took me to answer that question. God has this way of getting us to *really* come around. He transforms us from the inside out. It took many months of failure, sweat, and tears, but in the end, he set me free. Yes, it's enough. Jesus is enough for me. Whether things are good or bad, Jesus is always enough. I can honestly say God brought me to the place where if he wanted me to continue in that same situation, then for him, I'd do it.

And something wonderful happened: I experienced peace like I never had before. Trust me, I've got a long way to go, but I also had a long way to come. God gradually freed me from much of my need to achieve and my concern about being respected and esteemed. That peace was a gift from him and has made everything better since, regardless of whether my circumstances are good or bad. (There are pressures that come when things are going well, too, like worrying about when it will all end, or knowing that to whom much is given, much is expected.[9]) I don't want things to go badly, but I no longer need things to go well in order to be at peace, because God is enough.

No other person, not even in my imagination, has ever loved me like he has. "We love because he first loved us."[10] If loving God with all we have is the greatest thing we can do, I believe knowing that God loves us is the greatest thing we can know.

Reader, God loves you. If you were in a tight spot, captured by bloodthirsty men bent on torture, and your only hope was for someone to go on a suicide mission for you, Jesus would do it. Jesus would do it if he knew up front it would kill him. He would stick his neck out, dodge the bullets, risk his life. He would *give* his life for you. He'd walk into the torture chamber and say, "Torture me instead." I know he would because that's what he did. You've got to know this inside and out. Know it in your bones. You do not have to earn your way into God's love. He gives his love freely in Christ. Right now, this moment, without reservation or condition, he loves you perfectly.

Who else will love you like this?

For many of us, God's love can be a difficult thing to grasp, perhaps because of the way your parents loved you, or didn't, or because of the way your ex loved you, or didn't. The idea of God's love may not sit well with you if you've known Christian people who did not treat you as if they believed God loved you. Those words might have a hollow ring to them if your circumstances are difficult. *Well, if God loves me, he sure has a funny way of showing it.*

Circumstances change, but God doesn't. What Jesus did for us on the cross doesn't change. It doesn't matter what someone said to you or how someone treated you. Whether you feel like a success or a failure, healthy or sick, rich or poor. However you happen to feel at this moment, it is always true: God loves you.

Then It Was Clear

I can't imagine the disappointment Peter felt when they killed Jesus. He had given his whole life to this man. Peter trusted him. Everything had mattered so much when Jesus was in charge. He was in the inner circle of a fantastic spiritual revolution. But in the final hours of Jesus' life, Peter discovered he wasn't as committed as he thought he was. He had said he would die with Jesus, if that's what it came to, but Jesus knew better and predicted Peter would chicken out. Jesus said Peter would deny him three times before that day was over—before the rooster announced the morning sun.

When the accusers came, Peter's courage melted. Rather than risk being arrested himself, he denied knowing Jesus at all. Three times. Then the rooster crowed, and Peter realized what he was doing. He ran off and wept bitterly.

Later, Jesus was dead, and Peter was back in the boat earning his pittance by casting nets, knowing he would never get the chance to make it right.

But there was a lot more drag on the net than he'd expected. The whole crew strained against the ropes. There were dozens and *dozens* of huge fish. Peter squinted toward the shore. The man who'd called out to them had been right about where to cast the net. In a daze, Peter's mind worked backward to that first day, years before, when it all began.

John grabbed Peter's shoulder. "It is the Lord!"

Then it was clear. It was *him*.

How had he not recognized him? Peter had one thought: *Be with Jesus now.* When he heard the words "It is the Lord," his heart soared and his arms and legs moved automatically. He wrapped his clothes about him and scrambled forward and splashed into the sea. The last time he'd stepped out of a boat to get to Jesus, he'd walked on water. This time he floundered through it.

There on the beach, a fire crackled. The charred fish and toasted bread smelled delicious. The last time Peter had stood near a fire in Jesus' presence, he was surrounded by enemies accusing him. This time, he was with friends who believed as he did.

The others pulled the boat in, and Jesus shared a meal with his followers as he had many times before. In the past Jesus had miraculously fed thousands. This time, the Almighty Creator of the Universe made breakfast for a few friends.

Then he asked Peter what he asks each of us.

"Do you love me?"[11]

My experience teaching in Harlem helped me to understand the way God loves me. I had to accept his love as grace, because I didn't have anything else to stand on. I wasn't performing well, and I realized I'm not a very good person. I had to accept what I preach—that in Christ, God loves me regardless. I discovered that God's love is truly a gift and that he loves me more than I dared hope. But I also discovered that I loved God much less than I thought I did.

Receiving God's love costs me nothing. Loving God back is a different story.

This Is Personal

Love Is Something You Do

This Isn't for the Faint of Heart

I think we'd all agree that knowing, saying, feeling, and doing are not the same things. But that simple observation has some unsettling implications.

Knowing that loving God is the most important commandment does not necessarily mean we love him. Likewise, saying we love God or feeling love toward God does not necessarily mean we love him. Actually loving God is something different. Let me explain.

My wife likes surprises. It doesn't really matter what the surprise is, as long as it's a surprise. I'll occasionally try to plan a "surprise date." For us, that simply means she doesn't know what I've planned until we get where we're going, so it's a surprise to her. It's usually something simple—we might try

47

a new restaurant, see a movie, or view an exhibit. It doesn't really matter what we do, because the surprise is what makes it fun.

Years ago, before we were married and long before we moved here, I took her on a surprise date to New York City. She had no idea we were going there. As we pulled into the airport parking lot, she wondered why I would take her to eat at an airport restaurant. Given how little I earned at the time, it didn't occur to her I might actually have plane tickets.

When we boarded the plane, she began to realize this was more than the usual surprise date, but she still had no idea where we were going. When we landed in LaGuardia, she didn't know I had purchased tickets to see a musical, and she had no idea I had made arrangements with the production staff to take us onstage after the curtain call. When a silver-haired gentleman named Arturo approached us during the final applause in order to lead us onstage, she still didn't know I was about to ask her an important question. *The* question.

When I got down on one knee, again, she was surprised.

Of course, I can't remember anything I said even though I had practiced it for days. I do remember that I got a little support from the audience. A woman with a thick Spanish accent hollered over the excited chatter, "Say yes, sister! Say yes!" And I remember Lindsay knelt down to my level and put her arms around me. I remember her nodding and smiling. I remember that wonderful word, "yes." As I fumbled the ring out of my pocket, I heard that same woman, apparently surprised herself, call out, "He's got a ring, too!"

Different people experience love in different ways. Over the years, I've learned a little about how best to love my wife. She really appreciates whenever I do things around the house.

When I do the dishes, take the cat to the vet, or run an errand she was dreading, it's better than telling her "I love you." She likes that, too, but she feels loved when I serve.

Some people hate surprises. If Lindsay hated surprises, yet I insisted on proposing the way I did, I'm not sure you could say I loved her well in that moment. Or if what Lindsay really needed was for me to spend time with her but I just bought her gifts to get her off my back, could you even say that I loved her? Maybe I *felt* love toward her. Maybe I would *say* I loved her. But if I completely ignored what she liked or needed and just loved her however I felt like loving her, would I *actually* love her?

When Lindsay and I were in premarital counseling, our therapist said something to me I've never forgotten: "Love is something you do." More so than a feeling or desire, love is an action. Feelings come and go, but we can always choose to love. The Bible says, "Dear children, let us not love with words or speech but with actions and in truth."[1] In other words, just as our counselor said, love is something you do.

That should lead us to ask, How do we love God? If loving God is the most important thing we can do with our lives, then how do we do that? Maybe we *feel* love toward God. Maybe we would *say* we love him. But how do we *actually* love him?

There are a number of things that come to people's minds when asked this question. We express love to God through worship, right? Especially by singing songs together. So God really likes when we go to church. And when we spend time with him praying or reading our Bibles, he eats that stuff up. Oh yeah, and tithing. He loves it.

Not exactly. There's a sense in which we can love God in all those ways, but those things are secondary at best. Those things can be the expressions of what God really wants, but they aren't the heart of it. What God is after is much deeper and requires much more commitment. This isn't for the faint of heart, and it isn't for everybody.[2]

I can summarize our love for God in one simple word. It's a word that's about as popular these days as a root canal, and I don't particularly like the sound of it myself. Jesus said, "Anyone who loves me will obey my teaching."[3]

Obedience.

We get things backwards. We often think that when we obey God, he loves us more. We think we get points with him when we do what he asks. But God doesn't love the way we do. If God's love for me depended on what I did, I'd be doomed. You too. On the contrary, obedience is about how much *we* love *him.* If we willfully ignore something we know he wants, then we might *feel* like we love God, and we might *say* we love God, but do we *actually* love him?

"But if anyone obeys his word, love for God is truly made complete in them."[4] When it comes to loving God, love is something you do.

Beyond Balance

I kind of cut Jesus off in the last chapter. I wanted to emphasize the greatest commandment because I felt like we'd gotten so far off base and had been troubled by so many distractions and less important things. But in doing so, I interrupted Jesus, and we need to hear the rest of what he said, because it is so important to God that Jesus put it right up there with the greatest commandment. Jesus said it was equally important. It is so important to God, if we ignore it, we might as well quit all of that praying and worshiping and tithing stuff, too, because the hypocrisy drives him up a wall. This is something God takes personally.

When asked what the greatest commandment in the entire Bible was, Jesus replied, "'Love the Lord your God with all your heart and with all your soul and with all your mind.' This is the first and greatest commandment."[5] But he didn't stop there. He added, "And the second is like it: 'Love your neighbor as yourself.' All the Law and the Prophets hang on these two commandments."[6]

There are 613 commandments in the Old Testament.[7] Jesus said all of them hang on these two commands: love God and love others. If you want to understand the Bible, you must start with these. They are the CliffsNotes. If you were to flip the "Law and the Prophets" over to read the back of the book, the summary should say, "Love God with everything you have, and love your neighbor as yourself."

It's noteworthy that Jesus gave this second commandment without being asked for it. It's as if Jesus was saying, "Loving God is the most important thing, but I can't leave it at that or you'll be very confused about what that means. I can't just tell you the greatest commandment. You must understand the second commandment, as well." Jesus said the second commandment was "like" the first.[8] The New Living Translation captures the power of this moment. In it, Jesus says the second commandment is "equally important."

Notice Jesus didn't say, "Take care of yourself first, and then take care of your neighbor." He didn't say, "Love your neighbor with what's left over." He didn't say, "Love yourself and then your neighbor." Jesus said, "Love your neighbor *as yourself.*"

But he also didn't say, "Love your neighbor instead of your-self." He certainly didn't say, "Love your neighbor and hate yourself." He didn't even say, "Love your neighbor above yourself." Jesus said, "Love your neighbor *as yourself*."

Jesus did not despise himself. He took care of himself and even had fun. He was accused of being a glutton and drunkard, probably because he had such a great time with his disciples.[9] He took breaks to get away from the crowds and spend time with the Father.[10] Jesus taught and healed, but at some point he would always pack up and leave people unhealed and untaught. When it came time for Jesus to give his life, he begged the Father for another way to accomplish his purposes. Jesus was no masochist—he very much did not want to go through the pain. Jesus loved himself.

But he loved others as himself. In addition to his unwaver-ing fidelity to the Father, Jesus' willingness to endure terrible suffering was fueled by his love for others. Love is something you do, and it was with that measure of love that he loved us.

This is not a balancing act. We like to think that way, but it doesn't seem like Jesus lived a balanced life. I don't think he went around thinking, *Some for you, some for me.* Sometimes God encourages us to recoup, take care of ourselves, or nurse our wounds. Other times, God calls us to suffer and die. Strik-ing the right "balance" requires something beyond balance.

It requires obedience.

One of the reasons being involved in a church is critical to following God is because church is about others. Worship and teaching and all the things we do when we "go to church" are very important and help us grow in our love for God. But they aren't church. Church isn't a building, an event, or an organization. According to the Bible, church is a people—the "called out" people who are following Jesus together.[11] And part of what these people do is give us a broader perspective of God's heart.

Sometimes I need to take care of myself, and my church helps me do it. When Lindsay and I take a vacation, it's usually much needed. But we sometimes experience guilt because getting away always means leaving work undone. When my Christian friends affirm, "Yes, go, relax. You need to rest!" it makes the break that much better. The church sets us free.

Other times, I need my Christian friends to remind me to think of other people. It feels like everything in life, and especially in my own heart, conspires to keep me focused on myself—on my life, my stuff, my struggles, and my dreams. My friends at church need my love, too. They need prayers, encouragement, a listening ear. Being a part of church helps me to love others as myself.

You simply cannot be a Jesus-follower on your own. You can't obey much of the Bible that way. Jesus said, "If you keep my commands, you will remain in my love," and, "My command is this: Love each other as I have loved you."[12] Loving God and loving others are bound together. "For whoever does not love their brother and sister, whom they have seen, cannot love God, whom they have not seen."[13]

But the Righteous Will Be Perplexed

And there are others. As I write this and as you read it, there are people out there in need of our love. God cares so deeply for people that he takes our treatment of others personally. I've read the Bible from cover to cover, and I'm not sure I've ever heard Jesus speak as forcibly as he does when he tells us to care for others in Matthew 25.

When a man who is gentle by nature talks like this, it's frightening. It would be difficult to imagine a gentler man than Jesus. Isaiah described the Messiah's gentleness poetically: "A bruised reed he will not break, and a smoldering wick he will not snuff out."[14] Children wanted to be near him. Hurting people were drawn to him. But there are moments in Scripture when Jesus scares me, and this is one of them. It scared me the first time I read it. It scared me when we picked it apart in seminary. It scares me to write about it now.

Starting in verse 31, Jesus said that he would return at the end of ages in all his glory with all his angels. Angels are powerful and terrible heavenly beings. They are completely other from us. We cannot understand them, and the Bible doesn't try to help us do so. When people encountered an angel in the Bible, they were usually so terrified they fell to the ground and begged for mercy. If angels were careless in our presence, they could accidentally destroy us like a child touching a house of cards. The Bible says there are more angels than we can count.[15] Jesus will return with them all.

Jesus explained that he will then take his seat on his glorious throne and all the nations will be gathered before him. Billions and billions of people. Every man, woman, and child who ever took a breath. Plato, Genghis Kahn, Napoleon, the apostle Paul, Jimi Hendrix, me, and you. Not just the several billion who now live, but all the billions who lie in graves or on the ocean floor or whose ashes are scattered to the wind. We cannot even imagine a crowd like this. The largest church in the world, the most formidable army, and the vast movements of history will seem insignificant by comparison.

Like a shepherd separating the sheep from the goats, Jesus will separate the people. Every person who has ever drawn breath will receive a verdict.

Sheep to the right. Goats to the left.

To those on his right, the King will say,

Come, you who are blessed by my Father; take your inheritance, the kingdom prepared for you since the creation of the world. For I was hungry and you gave me something to eat, I was thirsty and you gave me something to drink, I was a stranger and you invited me in, I needed clothes and you clothed me, I was sick and you looked after me, I was in prison and you came to visit me.[16]

But the righteous will be perplexed by his words. They will ask, "Lord, when did we see you hungry and feed you, or thirsty and give you something to drink? When did we see you a stranger and invite you in, or needing clothes and clothe you? When did we see you sick or in prison and go to visit you?"[17]

To those on his left, the King will say,

Depart from me, you who are cursed, into the eternal fire prepared for the devil and his angels. For I was hungry and you gave me nothing to eat, I was thirsty and you gave me nothing to drink, I was a stranger and you did not invite me in, I needed clothes and you did not clothe me, I was sick and in prison and you did not look after me.[18]

They, too, will be perplexed. "When did we see you hungry or thirsty or a stranger or needing clothes or sick or in prison, and did not help you?"[19]

Jesus said everyone will get a similar response. To those on his right, the King will say, "Truly I tell you, whatever you did for one of the least of these brothers and sisters of mine, you did for me."[20] To those on his left, he will say, "Whatever you did not do for one of the least of these, you did not do for me."[21] Then Jesus concluded the lesson with these words: "Then they will go away to eternal punishment, but the righteous to eternal life."[22]

Jesus takes our treatment of others personally, especially our treatment of the poor and vulnerable. He says if we ignore the "least of these," we ignore him. And this wasn't the only time Jesus got riled up on behalf of vulnerable people. He said it would be better to have an enormous boulder tied to your neck and be thrown into the sea than to lead a child astray.[23] James 1:27 says, "Religion that God our Father accepts as pure and faultless is this: to look after orphans and widows in their distress and to keep oneself from being polluted by the world."

To love God, you must love others.

Pain Is the Price

Loving others like this, especially those in need, is difficult, messy, and often burdensome. There are feelings of accomplishment and significance that go along with it, but loving others just to feel something or get something isn't love at all. It doesn't work.

I want to shoot straight with you. If you choose to take Jesus' words seriously, expect trials, heartache, and the risk of danger. Expect also to sometimes feel very insignificant, because there is nothing flashy about loving the world the way Jesus commands.

That was one of the most surprising things about teaching in Harlem. The reality of serving those students was sometimes exciting, sometimes frightening, and sometimes comical. I grew to count on one or two novel experiences each day, whether it was a parent threatening to harm a student, a massive fight in the hallway, or, rarely, seeing a light bulb go on when a student understood something for the first time. Those moments were the spice of the work, but they weren't the meat and potatoes. The hard work of loving those students was the daily grind. I realized after a month of doing the work that no made-for-TV movie could capture it. You would need a forty-five-minute montage. You would need to show me erasing the chalkboard and resetting it between every class, day after day, over the months, over the years, as the scrawny city trees on the street below passed through all four seasons, blooming bright green, shriveling, and shedding the husks of their leaves. You would need to show me scrubbing graffiti off the desks, and then rescrubbing it, and then rescrubbing it. The montage would include long, boring, mandatory meetings. It would show me taking down and designing bulletin boards all over my classroom and in the hall, over and over and over again.

The montage would break in the middle to show me on the train, plunging through the underground of New York City toward home, slumped against the glass, vaguely watching the platforms whoosh by. The support pillars would flicker past, creating a strobe-light effect so that the movements of people on the platform looked jerky, like slow-motion break-dancers. Then at home it would show me hunched over the table, cranking out lesson plan after lesson plan, moving papers one at a time from the ungraded stack to the graded stack. And you would need to show me calling students' homes—talking to their mom, dad, grandmother, uncle, big sister, whoever they stayed with—tracking down cell phone numbers, leaving messages, calling back, over and over and over again.

This is not the easiest thing to do. This is not a call to a soft and sentimental kind of love. That feeling won't last, and you won't last if that's all that fuels you. Trust me, exhilarating feelings come to those who obey God, but that's secondary. This is a call to love the way Jesus loves, which means dying for others. "This is how we know what love is: Jesus Christ laid down his life for us. And we ought to lay down our lives for our brothers and sisters."[24] For many believers throughout history, this dying happened all at once in martyrdom. But for most of us, we give our lives bit by bit, every day, as "a living sacrifice."[25] Pain is the price of love in a sinful world.

It's easy to feel ready to love others until you get into the thick of it, and then you run into all kinds of things. People are ungrateful. They take your help and hurt you or others with it. People will sometimes treat you exactly the way we often treat God, glad for his help while ignoring his advice at our own peril. Thank God he loves us regardless.

If you actually intend to love others the way God wants you to but do it in your own strength or for their sake, you won't last. But what about for Jesus? After what he did for you, will you love others for him? Jesus takes our treatment of others personally. When you see someone in need and meet their need, you are doing that for Jesus.

It Happens Just Past a Man's Limits

Some days I could go into that awful school and deal with all the stress for the sake of the kids. Some days I couldn't. On those days, I did it for Jesus.

I wrote the following words in my blog about six months into my first year teaching in Harlem. Please excuse the choppy sentences and careless punctuation. During that year I let my blog posts just pour out and tried not to censor myself. I wrote for therapy, not for an audience. Here's what I wrote:

I quit Friday.

It started first thing in the morning. I had a really bad interaction with one of my 8th-graders as we were coming up from the gym to first period, and it was downhill from there.

This class of 8th-graders is notorious—the nastiest in the school. If you've been reading since the beginning of the school year, you're already familiar with some of them. You read about the one who was arrested for slamming me against the wall when the class rushed the door. You read about "Bill," who has since been involuntarily transferred out of the school for threatening my wife. You read about the kid who slapped my clip board out of my hand.

At the beginning of the year, this is the class that stole stuff from me (repeatedly), cursed me, trashed my room, ripped up books and materials, and banded together to protect each other from consequences by lying.

Somehow I had managed to get a level of rapport/respect with them where that kind of stuff wasn't happening. I was even getting quite a bit of work out of them, and I think they've been learning.

But Friday it was like flashbacks to September. Stealing stuff off my desk. Overturning chairs. A kid threw a book. Completely uncooperative, etc. I have them for three periods on Friday, and that was one too many. At the end of the third, I had had my fill.

God may not . . . but a man, my friends, has a limit.

I walked over to my closet, popped the padlock, grabbed my bag, hung my coat over my arm, and strode out of the building.

One of my 7th-grade classes (that I had the next period) was waiting in the hall to come inside, and they were actually kind of sweet. They ran after me down the hall. "Mr. Travis? Where are you going?" "What happened?" "You leavin'?" They chased me down the stairs to the door outside and called after me. I distinctly heard a voice from among the rest call out, "Don't give up on us!"

Which almost penetrated my heart. Almost.

A block or two down the street, a dean from one of the other schools that meets in our building caught up with me. "I can't let you leave like this." We live on the same part of the island, and I know him from taking the same train in the mornings.

Then one of our deans caught up, and together they managed to talk me down—at least into coming back in and sitting in an office and cooling off. I was so angry. The only place in God's creation where kids can act their worst and not face the natural consequences for it is in the public schools. It's infuriating.

But I did come back in. I did cool off. I even returned to teach my 7th-graders. Some of them had written really sweet things on the chalkboard about missing me and hoping I would come back.

And I'm pretty sure I'm going in tomorrow. I have told them that I wasn't going to leave—that I would stay to the end of the year. And I value my word, considerably (though the value I place on it, my friends, has a limit).

And I know what I need to do if it's going to work at all.

It doesn't really matter what the right thing to do is because I know what I need to do. So much of life is like that—you think it's about right and wrong, but it isn't. It's about what's True. It's about what is and what isn't.

And here's what is (I've searched for wisdom, and here's the only thing that can work): I have to apologize. I have to apologize for the tone I used with them. I have to apologize for giving up. I need to extend grace, and I need to receive it.

I have to let them know it's a new day, and that I never hold a grudge—that we can start over like it never happened. And while some of them are taller than I am, inside, they're children. And so, unlike adults, they'll believe me.

I thought that I had died to myself when I threw in my chips and gave my life to God. I hadn't. I received the new life, and that was wonderful. But the dying had only begun. It's gritty; it's ugly; it's painful.

The dying happens, well . . . it happens just past a man's limits.

I intend to finish this year. But it's gonna kill me.

Insignificant

We Serve a Servant God

So Behold the Master

Imagine you were rooting around in your attic or at a flea market and you found an old lamp caked with dust. You grabbed your sleeve to wipe the grime and, without thinking, rubbed its side three times. Blue smoke swirled from the spout and materialized into a wish-granting genie. What would you wish for?

If you've ever discussed that question in a group of people, you may have noticed that something similar always happens. At first, people wish for money, power, toys, fame, or for their dreams to come true. Then someone inevitably says they'd wish for more wishes, which, of course, everyone agrees you cannot do. But then at some point there's always that one gentle soul in the bunch who says they'd wish for world peace.

Then everyone else, perhaps feeling a little rebuked, begins channeling Mother Teresa, aiming for the most altruistic wish, and a subtle competition ensues. "I'd cure cancer" or "I'd feed all the hungry children." The guy who answered first (ahem, *me*) is left looking like a complete jerk with his personal resort island, ability to fly, and lifetime supply of Dr Pepper.

I'm going somewhere with this, so stick with me. Let me try to ask that same question in a slightly more realistic way: If you hit the lottery today and became an instant multi-millionaire, what would you do?

I'd probably buy an apartment in Manhattan so I could stop paying rent. I'd take my wife on a vacation. I know I'd take care of my family. I'd try to make some people's dreams come true—help them start a business, get a degree, take a trip to visit family. I'd certainly have some charitable plans, too, especially for the church I'm currently pastoring. There's no question I'd work for free if I could. And I'd give as much as I could to some of the mission work we're involved in. If I were a millionaire, that would be a lot.

Let me ask it again this way: What if you were a "big shot"? If you were famous or powerful, the sort of person people followed, what would you do? Imagine you were a business mogul, a celebrity, or the minister of a massive church. Or what if you were the president of the United States, in charge of the better part of the world's resources and military, what would you change?

Let me stretch it just a little further. What if God visited you today and said, "Here. It's all yours. Everything. I put it all under your feet. Anything you want done. The universe will be your servant. Just speak, and it will respond."

You may be more others-centered than I am. Maybe you wouldn't give any thought to yourself or your own loved ones. Maybe you'd give that winning lottery ticket away without even cashing it. Maybe you'd use your fame or your power to feed people, cure people, protect people. I imagine I would feel selfish and small when I saw how loving some of you would be.

But I'd bet anything you wouldn't do what Jesus did.

God put everything under his feet. The Father made the entire universe subject to him. Jesus had it all, and he knew it. "Jesus knew that the Father had put all things under his power."[1] So he cured all disease, ended all suffering, erased all evil, wiped away every tear. He answered all our prayers. He stopped the nonsense and rebellion and asserted his lordship.

No. Not this God.

"Jesus knew that the Father had put all things under his power . . . so he got up from the meal, took off his outer clothing, and wrapped a towel around his waist. After that, he poured water into a basin and began to wash his disciples' feet, drying them with the towel that was wrapped around him."[2]

Love is what God is after, and power has no power to prompt love. So behold the Master of the Universe, the Ancient of Days, the Lord of Heaven's Armies: Jesus Christ the Foot Washer.

You Don't Know What You Are Asking

If love is the goal, power doesn't get us very far. This is not the easiest thing to understand. Once we start to get our minds around it, it almost immediately slips away. It's no surprise Jesus' disciples had difficulty keeping up with him even after following him so closely for years. Any of us would have, too.

James and John, the sons of Zebedee, were a couple of characters. That's really the only way to describe them. Since the moment they left their father in the fishing boat to follow Jesus, they must have added an interesting flavor to his band of followers. Jesus called them the "sons of thunder."[3] Some traditions say it was because of their loud and boisterous nature, others because of their temper. We know they were working-class men, fishermen, and likely a little rough around the edges. I picture a couple of bouncers. They certainly acted the part. Once while traveling toward Jerusalem, when it was almost time for Jesus to give his life for us, Jesus sent some ahead to make preparations in a Samaritan village. But the villagers did not welcome them. When the sons of thunder heard about this affront, they asked Jesus, "Lord, do you want us to call fire down from heaven to destroy them?"[4]

Whoa. Just a little excessive.

Jesus rebuked them. His response was simply to move along to a different village.

Knowing a little about what sort of men these two were makes it even funnier that they let their mom go to bat for them in Matthew 20:20–28. They left their dad behind in the boat, but apparently Mom tagged along with Jesus, at least from time to time. One day, she came to Jesus with her sons and asked a favor of him.

"What is it you want?" asked Jesus.

Thunder Mom said, "Grant that one of these sons of mine may sit at your right and the other at your left in your kingdom." In other words, she said, "Please promote my boys to the top positions in your kingdom." I wonder whether her sons felt embarrassed.

"You don't know what you are asking," Jesus said to them. "Can you drink the cup I am going to drink?"

"We can," they answered.

Jesus said to them, "You will indeed drink from my cup, but to sit at my right or left is not for me to grant. These places belong to those for whom they have been prepared by my Father."

They didn't know what they were asking, and Jesus' words proved true. Later, when this new movement of Christ-followers gained momentum, King Herod arrested many of them. They executed James by the sword.[5]

But the other disciples didn't understand, either, because when they heard about this, they were indignant. Jesus called them all together and explained something we need to understand today: "You know that the rulers of the Gentiles lord it over them, and their high officials exercise authority over them. Not so with you. Instead, whoever wants to become great among you must be your servant, and whoever wants to be first must be your slave—just as the Son of Man did not come to be served, but to serve, and to give his life as a ransom for many" (Matthew 20:25–28).

This wasn't the first time Jesus explained this to them. Read through the Gospels, and it seems like he was constantly explaining this. Things don't work in the kingdom of God as they do in the world. Sinners, poor people, sick people, slaves, oppressed people like women, children, and minorities—they belong in the kingdom of God. One time Jesus said it was actually harder for rich people to get into heaven than it is for poor people. This must have felt like a smack in the face to people who took it for granted that rich people are rich because God had blessed them and they deserved it (a notion that is, unfortunately, just as popular today). But Jesus said prostitutes and dishonest government officials would enter the kingdom of heaven before the religious leaders did.[6]

Confused, his disciples asked, "Who, then, is the greatest in the kingdom of heaven?"

Jesus called a little child to him and explained, "Unless you change and become like little children, you will never enter the kingdom of heaven."[7]

Weaker, Smaller, and More Dependent

The greatest people in God's eyes are insignificant to the world. If you want to be like God, you must be a servant to all. And if you want to enter the kingdom of heaven, you must change and become like little children. Isn't that the opposite of what we want? I want God to make me strong, confident, independent, and powerful. Jesus says I must be weak, small, and dependent upon him.

I used to think I knew what I was doing. I was on staff at a church and I had developed some ministry competence. I was an adequate speaker, and I knew that if I put time into studying and preparing like they taught me in seminary, I could preach a message that would "work"—meaning it wouldn't overly irritate anyone and people wouldn't fall asleep. It wasn't until much later in life when I tried to actually change people's hearts and lives through preaching that I realized how hopelessly inadequate to the task I am. I know now I can do nothing on my own. Teaching in Harlem taught me that.

During that first awful year, I suppose I became a better teacher. If you looked in from the outside and compared my skill as a teacher from one year to the next, you might conclude that I had really improved. But I don't see it that way. To me, I became weaker, smaller, and more dependent upon God, and some cool things started to happen.

But God dragged me into it kicking and screaming, and it was painful. When I returned from spring break, there were ten weeks remaining in that first school year. I thought about those ten weeks as ten rounds of a boxing match. From the comfort of a day off, ten weeks doesn't sound like much. Of course, neither does a three-minute round until you try it. Have you ever tried to box for three minutes? Ever tried to just hit a heavy bag for three minutes? If you aren't conditioned and you go all out, it'll make you sick. Getting through one day teaching in that environment felt like a battle. Lasting until Friday often felt impossible. I regularly called my wife for a pep talk just to get through one more class.

In Round One I came out swinging. All the phone calling and home visits and painstaking consistency was apparently paying off. I'd never enjoyed so much peace and control in my classroom. My management reflexes were honed, and I couldn't believe how wonderful it was when the students were the ones doing the hard work.

I enjoyed another week of the same in Round Two, and I was beside myself, jumping up on the turnbuckles and raising my gloves to the roaring crowds. Had I actually figured this job out?

Nope. In Round Three I started to tire and realized I had only been well rested from the break.

Then in Round Four, the scores for the New York State exams came back, and my seventh-graders did so poorly I was crushed. Most of them actually lost ground academically. I mean, they improved, but not a full grade level. I know the environment hindered me more than helped me, but who cares? I failed. The injustice of the American public school system's achievement gap reveled in another victory.

But while I took a good shot on one cheek, I stood back up, spit out a tooth, and turned the other. My eighth-graders did *well*. Out of the twenty-six students, eighteen of them improved *more* than a grade level.

Rounds Five, Six, Seven, and Eight rolled by, one bell at a time. That school and I were back and forth, pacing and growling, throwing punches and taking them. Round Nine closed with us pinned against the ropes, clinging to one another, dizzy and gulping air.

In Round Ten, the final week of the school year, I had a rematch with the eighth-grade arm-wrestling champion. Earlier in the year I had earned a lot of respect from the older boys by dominating this kid. This kid was three inches taller than me and had me by sixty pounds. I won that time because I was fit, and I'd successfully waged an effective psychological war, working days in advance to convince him "old muscle" was full of grit and poison and rusty nails, and it didn't matter how big he was, he didn't stand a chance. It worked. He was psyched out and I beat him. Not this time, though. I had lost about fifteen pounds over the course of that first year while he apparently kept drinking milk. I watched, powerless to stop it, as he slowly pressed my knuckles into the desk.

My defeat did not hinder the celebration at all. We had pizza and ice cream, and Lindsay and I made Rice Krispies

Treats. Many of my students had never had one before. I also learned that the gelatin in the marshmallow was a pork product forbidden to my Muslim students, an insensitive oversight I wouldn't repeat.

As that final bell drew near, I began to sense the question, almost a taunt, in strange places. It showed up in the eyes of my students when I returned their portfolios to them, or when I hugged them good-bye. I'd catch a whisper of it in the screech of the subway car, or amid the city noises as I sat out on my fire escape, praying.

It asked, "Rematch?"

By this time I knew the next chapter in my life involved planting a church in New York City. I intended to contribute one more year teaching in NYC public schools, so I kept asking myself, with just one year to contribute, where can I have the most impact? All practical wisdom and good sense and sound judgment screamed, "Not here!"

But there was this teeny tiny voice, so quiet I could barely sense the tickle of it, so unassuming it was easy to ignore if I wanted to. I could hear it through the din of the cursing, fighting children behind me, somehow softly cutting through. Back in my corner, was that my manager?

"Chris. Fight."

But That's Getting Into Year Two

When I decided to come back to that same school for a second year, it might have been the stupidest decision I ever made. I had nothing to gain and everything to lose. It's also one of the very few times in my life when I am certain I did what God asked me to do.

That first year was the worst and most difficult year of my life. I saw more blood and tears, including my own, than I had in the entire decade before it. I don't think a day went by when I didn't witness something awful or hear several X-rated statements. The good days were the days when I wasn't on the receiving end of them. I woke in the middle of the night from nightmares of mean-spirited students throwing things at me—then I'd go to school where mean-spirited students threw things at me. I was powerless, ineffective, stressed, depressed, and wasn't doing anybody any good. Dark things rose in my soul. I found in my heart a disappointing mix of hatred, bitterness, and a desire for revenge, all caged restlessly, ready to spring forth the moment provocation turned the key. The whole experience seemed to be making me less and less like Jesus, in spite of my best efforts to be like him. I was very far from the notion of the victorious Christian I had in my mind. I was not a candidate for a made-for-TV movie about teaching in a tough school. I was the poster child for failure.

But sometimes God would give me a glimpse of how he was at work. Once, as I was dismissing class, I noticed a student facing the wall, and I could tell by her posture she was weeping. As I was giving orders about how to clean up and line up, I drew near to her and said under my breath, "Could you stick around for a moment. You're not in trouble."

Once everyone had left, I asked, "Someone was making fun of you?"

"Yeah."

"Well, you don't have to tell me who, but what was it about?"

She hung her head. "'Cause they weighed us in gym class, and I'm in the two hundreds. The heaviest in class, so they sayin' stuff."

I sighed. "Look at me. *I* think that you are beautiful. You are in middle school. That means no matter what, kids are going to make fun of you. If it wasn't that, it would be your shoes. Or because your brother's ugly. Or anything else. There's no getting out of it. But it doesn't make any of it true. Don't give whatever they've said another thought."

Other times, these moments were funny.

"Angelo, what's it gonna take for you to behave today?"

"Tell me what you're doing over the break."

"That's it? You're easy . . . Well, my wife has been out of town for work, and she's coming back tonight. We're gonna spend the next couple days together just relaxing."

Angelo said, "Oh, so you're gonna . . ." and then he pantomimed copulation, convincingly.

I broke character and chuckled. Noticing that several other boys had tuned in, I said, "That's a bit personal, but let me just say this: Gentlemen, it is *good* to be married. *Good.* When you find that right woman, you marry her, and don't ever cheat on her. There's nothing better."

But the moments I can point to like these, when I had the chance to say something important, felt very infrequent. There often wasn't a whole lot to hang on to. From time to time, I clung to these words from Scripture, which served as a life preserver for me:

Endure hardship as discipline; God is treating you as his children. For what children are not disciplined by their father? If you are not disciplined—and everyone undergoes discipline— then you are not legitimate, not true sons and daughters at all. Moreover, we have all had human fathers who disciplined us and we respected them for it. How much more should we submit to the Father of spirits and live! They disciplined us for a little while as they thought best; but God disciplines us for our good, in order that we may share in his holiness. No discipline seems pleasant at the time, but painful. Later on, however, it produces a harvest of righteousness and peace for those who have been trained by it.[8]

It was the last sentence that got me through. Discipline produces a harvest of peace and righteousness. I would think, *Chris, what would you trade for peace and righteousness? What could be worth more?* And then I would endure the hardship, believing God loves me as a good father does.

I had to change, though, and become like a child. I found out firsthand what it means that God's strength is made perfect in weakness.[9] I had no idea how rich the harvest of peace would be or how good some things would get. I never would have dared dream it. But that's getting into year two.

A Surprising Promise

I wonder what went through Judas' mind when Jesus stooped to wash his feet. Honestly, I think Judas hated him for it. During the meal that followed, Judas got up from the table and betrayed him to religious leaders who were hungry for Jesus' blood. I think Judas looked down his nose at the Servant King and hated him for his love. This was not the King they were waiting for. Not this gentle miracle worker. Not this foot washer. Judas didn't want a God who would overturn the power structures of our world. He didn't want a kingdom without haves and have-nots. Judas wanted a God who would make him one of the haves.

I wonder what went through Jesus' mind as he washed Judas' feet and lovingly dried them. Did Jesus pray for him?

Father, please forgive Judas for what he has planned. He does not know what he's doing. If he did, it certainly wasn't the only time he would pray like that.[10]

Judas walked closely with Jesus for years. He understood who Jesus was and what he came to accomplish as well as any of us. And Judas said, "No thanks."

What about you?

Jesus is who he is. Do you want this Servant King? His priority is not to prove you right or fix your problems. His priority is love. Is this the God for you, or are you holding out for a conquering king? Would you be among those demanding a miracle in order to believe? Would you call out to Jesus on the cross, "Let him save himself if he is God's Messiah"?[11]

If you want a god who will make you a winner in this world and assert all your rights, then Jesus is not the god for you. In this broken, love-barren world of win-lose, following Jesus often means losing. It often means coming in last. Loving others means serving them. It certainly meant that for Jesus himself.

It would have taken several minutes to wash all of his disciples' feet. For several minutes, they watched. They watched this man who had chosen them, simple working men, to be the first disciples of *the* great spiritual revolution in history. Jesus had loved them, fed them, taught them, and encouraged them for years. Jesus wielded the power to command demons, command nature, and command obedience, but with a startlingly soft touch. He was much more than divine. He was also a good friend. And there he stooped, in his undergarment, the towel at his waist growing grimier with each clean foot. John 13:12–16 closes the scene:

When he had finished washing their feet, he put on his clothes and returned to his place. "Do you understand what I have done for you?" he asked them. "You call me 'Teacher' and 'Lord,' and rightly so, for that is what I am. Now that I, your Lord and Teacher, have washed your feet, you also should wash one another's feet. I have set you an example that you should do as I have done for you. Very truly I tell you, no servant is greater than his master, nor is a messenger greater than the one who sent him."

Jesus concluded this teaching with a surprising promise: "Now that you know these things, you will be blessed if you do them."[12]

This win-lose world is passing away, and quickly. I can barely believe how much of my life is already over. It's so fleeting. We'll all be in the grave before we know it. So much of what we think matters is temporary and ultimately insignificant. But what matters to God matters forever. What he offers is so much better than "being right" or "winning" or "success" that it makes those idols appear laughable. There is a new world coming, and we can only begin to imagine it. It's as if we were born and raised in a prison cell and someone mailed us a postcard from the beach. It looks beautiful all right, but we have no idea what it really is. If we knew that lying on the sun-warmed sand felt like a massage, and that cool waves felt like a mother rocking a child; if we knew the smell of the ocean wind and the sparkle of the starlit sky; if we knew the taste of fresh coconut and the freedom to go wherever we wanted whenever we wanted; if our color-starved eyes could see past the gray brick and our stiff muscles could imagine the freedom to run with no walls—the longing for it all would break our hearts. The hope deferred would kill us where we stood. There's not much we can do on this side of the grave to understand it all, beyond knowing that it's too wonderful to grasp.

There are some postcards from the beach in the Bible, though, and we should at least look at them. We will before this book is through.

The first half of this book has been mostly about what we need to know. God puts himself last for us. What God wants most from us is our love. We love God by loving others. If you want to be great in God's eyes, you must be a servant. We need to know these things, but now it's time to consider what we should do about it.

Reader, you matter in the surprising way God is changing the world. The rest of this book will attempt to show you how.

What Only God Can Do

Dependence Is the Path to Power

Without Looking to the Right or to the Left

I'm not sure which is worse, being sucker-punched or knowing you're going to be punched. I entered my second year of teaching hardened for the fight, ready to take it on the chin. The day before the students came, we had mandatory professional development. I quietly endured a day full of meetings about how to fill out incident reports while the words floated over top of me.

". . . lowest performing school in all of Manhattan academically . . ."

". . . highest number of student injuries per capita . . ."

I tried not to be cynical. I tried to encourage the new teachers that they'd make it somehow. Inwardly, I bit down on my mouth guard and waited for the hits to start coming.

The next morning, I choked my tie up tight, jerked the lapel of my jacket taut, and marched down to the gym to pick up my class. My shoes shone with polish. I looked straight ahead on the way down the stairs, heels clicking rhythmically. My feet had the number of steps in each flight memorized. As I pushed the door open into the gym, I transformed my face, my eyes, my energy, and became Mr. You-never-know-*what-this-scary-white-man-might-do-to-make-you-miserable-if-you-don't-do-what-he-says* Travis.

Then I plunged into the crowd. Without looking to the right or to the left, I blazed a trail through the chaos of a hundred kids, some taller than me, some acting tough, most running and chattering. Several of my homeroom students huddled near where our class number was posted on the wall, trying to stay out of the way. This year I had sixth-graders, and they looked tiny.

"Line up here," I said and pointed. They did. I was a little surprised by this, but you never would have known it from the hardness in my face.

Then I noticed that one little girl was trembling. It was a little chilly out, so I asked, "Are you cold?"

"No, I'm just nervous."

My heart melted. This is what sixth-graders are supposed to be like. Not these wannabe gangsters with their boxers hanging out, grabbing their crotches and smacking each other, yelling obscenities.

I couldn't afford to be soft, though—at least not for a few months, if ever. "You have nothing to fear," I lied, stone-faced. "My name is Mr. Travis. I am your homeroom teacher. I will make sure you know what to do."

The rest of the day went so well I could hardly believe it.

I made my students take diagnostic tests to assess their prior knowledge, and you could have heard a pin drop. The next day, the same. And the next. Teachers I didn't even know stopped by the class to commend us on "how on point" we were. Teachers from other schools somehow knew my name. The administrators were pleased.

It felt like someone just gave me ten free months. It felt like a prison sentence had been forgiven. When I came home one night full of energy and mental clarity to get some work done, I froze, suddenly amazed. The year before, things were so ugly and violent that I'd come home utterly exhausted, struggling to conjure even simple words to hold a conversation with my wife. But here I was, at home, thinking clearly. The possibilities! I began to imagine what I could accomplish with energy in the evenings and felt like pinching myself.

A few things had changed for me that I could name, and there were probably a hundred other things I'm not aware of, all contributing to the difference. Of course, I had changed. I learned how to do the job, and I was really working at it. In the first two weeks of the school year, I made a positive contact with almost all of my students' parents. At other schools that might have been a simple matter of picking up the phone. At this school, tracking down parents or guardians meant serious detective work. When I got in touch with someone, I turned up the charm and built bridges and did whatever I had to do to get them on my side.

I was also much stricter on conduct. Having seen the miles and miles kids take if you give an inch, I gave nothing. If you said a curse word in my presence, I treated it as if you'd punched a baby in the face. Three weeks into the school year, I could actually count on one hand the number of curse words I had heard in my room. I simply cannot write anything that can express what a change that was. I had grown used to students regularly screaming obscenities in my face. And now, nothing.

I also learned how to explain things better, how to use my facial expressions instead of my words, how the right kind of whisper is more powerful than shouting. I learned most of their tricks, too. I could tell by the angle of a kid's arms that they were texting underneath the desk. I learned how to spot the leaders and the troublemakers and the predators. I was better at determining whether a kid needed to be encouraged, challenged, or called out in front of his peers in order to curb dangerous behavior.

Things had changed, and I had changed, but that didn't quite explain it. There was something else going on.

It Took Me a While to Determine the Cause

The school was as crazy as ever (it stayed in operation only one more year after I left before the city successfully shut it down). But in the midst of the chaos, there was a new power at work. My words made things happen, and I wasn't even sure why. Somehow I was able to motivate cooperative behavior and get the leaders on my side. And my kids were drawn to me. They wanted to spend their lunches with me. When they saw me on the street, they ran to chat with me. My girls would sprint down the block to give me a hug. There was something going on I couldn't explain. It was as if the universe were cooperating with me.

One morning, as my first-period class was settling into their warm-up math problems, I heard a commotion growing in the hallway. I stood up from my desk fast enough to startle my class in order to get everyone's eyes on me. "You will stay seated and continue working," I said. They did.

When I entered the hallway, I found over fifty students playing and chattering, unsupervised. This was exactly the sort of situation that could easily escalate into something terrible. There were two classes of students there. One was a class I taught, so I knew their names. But I didn't teach the other class. I looked to one of the girls I knew and asked, "Where are you supposed to be?"

"We're with Mr. Granit and they with Ms. Ormon, but they not here." I could see Mr. Granit's and Ms. Ormon's doors were closed and the lights were off. They could have been anywhere, responding to some kind of emergency or covering for someone else or who knows what.

To understand what happened next, you need to know something about how difficult it is to get middle school students to line up and quiet down, or to do anything for that matter. These students presented a special challenge because many did not respect authority on principle. I can't tell you the number of times a guest speaker or visiting teacher would storm out of our building, deeply frustrated that they couldn't get a word in over the din of students doing their own thing, shocked that a student would actually get up and dance in front of them or invite them to do something X-rated. Teachers (or pastors, like me) who are used to people giving them respect because of their position are crushed to discover their authority actually makes the kids want to *disrespect* them. Many of these kids are taught by their parents to distrust and resist authority, sometimes for good reasons. Many of their parents have witnessed or been the victims of injustice at the hands of crooked police or city officials.

Getting students to line up and follow instructions is sort of a fundamental classroom management skill. They need to be able to do it in order to pass through the halls without disturbing others, and a good teacher needs them to do it so they can keep an eye on everyone in the class. Otherwise, you miss things that escalate, and kids get hurt. Or they'll miss out on important opportunities. If they can't line up and listen to instructions, they'll never be able to take field trips and navigate the streets of New York City or the subway system. But it is a very difficult thing to teach students to do. During my first year, my students were a mob, constantly playing, hitting each other, and running off.

Many of these kids in the hallway right now knew me only by reputation, if at all, and they were making way too much noise to hear me. I stood up tall and glared down the hall at this frenzy of wild students. I said to myself, *Mr. Travis decides how things work around here, and they will obey me.* I projected the energy of affront and indignation, and I know it showed on my face.

One by one, they noticed. "Ooh . . . Mr. Travis watchin'." They nudged each other, shushed each other, stopped and stared. After several moments, they were all silent and fell still. I glared at fifty pairs of eyes. When they were still and silent, I spoke slowly.

"You . . . are disrupting . . . education."

I stared.

"Now, without saying *one single word*," I said, raising my voice on those last three words to a volume somewhere between street-preacher and roar. Students' eyes widened.

Then I let my voice fall so soft they had to lean in to hear it. "Please form two lines. Gentlemen, against the wall. Ladies, beside them."

I could not believe my eyes when dozens of students silently did what I asked. I almost broke character and chuckled. It was a sight to see. It felt like a mountain uprooted itself and jumped into the sea just because I told it to. I couldn't believe it. Of course, I didn't let them see that on my face. Outwardly, I looked as if I expected the bulletin boards to peel themselves off the walls and line up, too.

"I don't know why Mr. Granit and Ms. Ormon are delayed. I'm sorry for that. Until they arrive, you will be patient and respectful." I smiled and went back into my room. Every few minutes I paused the lesson and stepped out into the hallway to see if they were patient and respectful. They were.

This strange power wasn't just with the students, either. With the administration, I felt like Joseph working under Pharoah. I cannot tell you the number of times that coincidences lined up in such a way that I looked like an absolute master. At any given time, there was an impossible, crushing list of expectations on us. There was no way anyone could accomplish all that teachers were asked to do. Never in my worst days of ministry have I encountered such a devastating workload or such an outrageous amount of paper work. But over and over again I would get this sense—a gut feeling—that I needed to do *this particular thing*. I knew I couldn't get half of all that was expected of me done, but I sensed that I really needed to get my data binder in order, organizing all of my students' test histories with individual plans for remediation. Then that same afternoon there would be a surprise inspection of our data binders, and I'd be the one teacher with a perfect example. Or on another day I put brand-new, great-looking student work up on all my bulletin boards, and there was a surprise inspection to check how recent the work in our displays was. After this sort of thing happened about a dozen times, the administration thought I was a perfect teacher and completely backed off me.

But I wasn't! If they had done a surprise inspection for anything else, they would have found me in total disarray, unprepared, looking unprofessional and incompetent. Somehow, over and over again, the one thing I managed to complete was the one thing they asked for.

It took me a while to determine the cause of all this.

Reader, it was *him*.

You Will Begin to Feel Inadequate

Throughout the course of that first year, I was so inadequate that I started to depend upon God in ways I never had before. It sounds counterintuitive, but one of the ways I depended on God was by becoming incredibly disciplined. For example, I had to get a full night's sleep every night, even if that meant going to bed while the sun was still up. I ate right. I exercised. I protected rest vigilantly. I made sure Lindsay and I spent time together. And I prayed every morning and throughout the day.

Now, before you get the wrong idea about this, I didn't do all this because I'm an ultra-disciplined person. I had no choice. If I skipped sleep, a fight would break out in my room because I'd have missed the subtle stirrings that always preceded violence. Yes, I suppose I was a disciplined person. God disciplined me. If I was off even a little, I'd miss something. I'd miss that every time I turned my back, Jamal would silently threaten to gather his friends and jump Jeffrey after school. I'd miss the growing affront, the shadow of murder in Jeffrey's eyes. Then, when Jeffrey flipped his desk over, or ripped his shirt off, or charged Jamal, seemingly out of nowhere, we'd all pay for it. Even when I was at the very top of my game, this sort of thing would happen from time to time. But if I was off by even a little, it was almost guaranteed.

I often felt like I was in way over my head. It felt like I never knew what to do, never knew what to say, never knew how to explain things. I prayed like I had never prayed before, not because I'm some kind of prayer warrior or because I'm super-spiritual, but because I couldn't get it right and had nowhere else to turn. I didn't know what to say to stop a fight from happening. I didn't know how to shut down a heckler. I didn't know how to make kids feel safe when there were predators around. I didn't know how to motivate kids to want to learn or how to cast a vision for how education could possibly matter to them. I didn't know how to do most of what I was trying to do, and I still don't. Instead, I prayed. I asked other people to pray for me. I had to.

Your work and your life might be much different from mine, but we all have moments when we're in over our head. Whether you are trying to raise a teenager, maintain integrity within an industry peppered with ethical landmines, salvage an ailing relationship, survive cancer, or actually get an education while everyone else is partying, I'm sure you've felt it. It's one thing to keep your head down, stay out of trouble, and collect your paycheck. Anybody with resolve can pull that off. If you want to do something that actually matters, there's good news and bad news: you can't. There are some things only God can do.

First: What's There

I don't think it was a coincidence that these changes began after months of praying through "The Lord's Prayer." Of course, there's nothing magical about praying any particular words in any particular way. But sometimes I'll hear people say things like, "Prayer is just talking to God; there's no right or wrong way to do it." In one way that's true. God wants us to be honest, knows what we need even before we ask him, and wants a relationship with us.[1] We don't need church jargon or flowery language. Our own words are best.

But I think sometimes when we say that, we secretly mean, "I don't need to learn anything about prayer." And that is nonsense. That would be like me saying, "I don't need to learn anything about how to communicate with my wife." I don't think it would serve our relationship very well if that were my attitude. And we're not talking about communicating with a human here. We're talking about communicating with the God of the Universe.

Jesus' disciples recognized they had much to learn about prayer. One day after Jesus returned from praying, one of his disciples said, "Lord, teach us to pray."[2] Jesus did not say, "There's nothing to know. Just go talk to God." Jesus taught them how to pray. He shared an example prayer, a template that we now call "The Lord's Prayer." This prayer appears more than once in Scripture, with minor variations to the wording (which shows that it's not about getting the words right, but about concepts). Most of us can recite the words of this prayer by heart. Even if you're only just beginning to explore faith, you've probably heard it at enough weddings and funerals, and in movies and TV, to get pretty close. The version you remember might have "thy" and "thou" instead of "your," but the idea's the same. Jesus said:

> This then, is how you should pray:
>   "Our Father in heaven,
>   hallowed be your name,
>   your kingdom come,
>   your will be done,
>   on earth as it is in heaven.
>   Give us today our daily bread.
>   And forgive us our debts,
>   as we also have forgiven our debtors.
>   And lead us not into temptation,
>   but deliver us from the evil one."[3]

There is too much in this prayer for us to unpack it all. Every word matters. The words *Father* and *hallowed* say so much about who we're talking to—our God is a loving Father and the Holy One. Praying for "daily" bread says something important about making these conversations a daily experience. And notice the importance Jesus places on forgiveness and on dependence upon God, rather than self, to avoid temptation. We could fill an entire book with insights from this prayer, and there are many good books that do just that. Whether you read them or not, if you begin to use this prayer as a template to think through your conversations with God, you will discover more and more meaning in these words.

For our purposes, there are two things I want to point out. The first is something that is conspicuously present in this prayer that we often ignore. The second is something that is conspicuously absent but that tends to dominate our prayers anyway.

First, what's there. Jesus taught us to pray, "Your kingdom come, your will be done, on earth as it is in heaven." In other words, in prayer we first align ourselves with God's will and not the other way around. According to Jesus, prayer is not about getting God to do what we want as much as it is figuring out what he wants. Friends, I cannot overstate the importance of praying like this. When Jesus' disciples asked him to teach them how to pray, Jesus said to start by recognizing who God is, praising him, and submitting to his will. Pray this way first before moving on to other things.

And praying like this takes up half the prayer! It's as if Jesus said, "Okay, if you want to know how to pray like I do, then you need to start out by praying for God's will, and that should be at least *half* the conversation." This is the first thing we must come to terms with if we want our lives to be significant. Trying to get God to do our will is small and lonely. Asking God to sweep us up into his will, to give us what we need so we can do what he wants—this leads to a life that matters.

In practice, you will find you know God's will a whole lot better than you think you do. Let's imagine you are praying in the morning before you start your day. Think through what you will face that day, and pray for God's will to be done first, not your own.

"Father, please help me to lead this meeting so that every voice is heard and wisdom prevails."

"Father, may your kingdom come in our home today. Help us support and encourage one another and be at peace with one another."

"Father, may your will be done today in my classroom. May it run the way it would if Jesus were teaching it. And not just my classroom, but every class in my school. And Father, may your will be done through every teacher in the NYC public school system, all thirty thousand of them. In every classroom in all the world, in every one-room schoolhouse in every remote village, may your will be done. In the hearts of every professor in every university in every nation, may your kingdom come. Move policy makers and curriculum writers and textbook publishers, school boards and administrators, all to the rhythms of your perfect will today."

We get tunnel vision as we focus on our tiny little worlds. Praying like this helps us lift our heads and see the horizon. It is only after recognizing who God is, praising him, and praying for *his* will and *his* kingdom, that Jesus teaches us to pray for our daily needs.

Instead of Praying

Second, look at what *isn't* there.

Reread Jesus' teaching on prayer and pay attention to the pronouns. "Our . . . your . . . your . . . your . . . us . . . our . . . we . . . our . . . us . . . us . . ." What's missing?

Here's a challenge: Try to pray every day for a month without using the words *I* or *me*. It's very difficult. I tried but couldn't do it perfectly. I had no idea how self-centered I was until I tried.

Of course, there's nothing wrong with praying for ourselves. Read through the example prayers in the Psalms and you'll find "I" all over the place. But it's noteworthy that when Jesus taught us to pray, he taught us to pray not only for ourselves but to identify with others. Give *us*. Forgive *us*. Deliver *us*.

There is an important principle about significance at work here. We mistakenly think that if we've got it all together and can stand on our own two feet and are truly independent, then we're powerful. But in reality, dependence is the path to power. Strength flows from a daily dependence on God and by identifying ourselves with others.

During my first year of teaching, my prayers were almost entirely self-centered. I was having such a difficult time, it was all I could manage. I prayed "please help me" and "please make this easier on me" and "please keep so-and-so home today so I don't have to deal with them." I was broken and hurting and I asked others to pray for me. I thought I mostly needed God to help me either get out of the situation or comfort me so I could handle it. I don't think God enjoyed seeing me in a difficult situation, but I think he was dreaming bigger things for me than I dared dream for myself. He actually wanted me to accomplish his will. It wasn't until the switch flipped in my mind and I began to focus my prayers on him and on others that I began to see some real power moving through me.

Before, I'd have been more likely to pray, "Lord, strengthen me so I can get through this day." Gradually, I began to pray, "Lord, strengthen me so I can accomplish what you have for me today."

Instead of praying, "Father, help me craft this lesson so they'll stay busy and not get out of hand," I began praying, "Father, help them understand. Show me how to present this so they'll get it."

Instead of, "I can't do this anymore. I need a break. Please make my kids behave," I prayed, "Father, you want my students to learn and feel safe in my room even more than I do. Show me how to lead them."

I began to pray for wisdom and the right words to break through. I began to pray that God would create opportunities for me to interact with the students about their lives. I began to pray not just for what I needed but for extra, and then some, so I'd have what it took to give and serve. I still prayed for myself, but something had shifted. I prayed less often for what I wanted and more often that God would give me what I needed to accomplish his will and to serve others well.

Praying like this is significant. If praying for your own children matters, then imagine what a difference it makes to pray for all the children in your neighborhood. Imagine how significant it is to pray not only for yourself and your dreams and your fears, but to also take some spiritual responsibility for others. If you have authority over anyone—if you are a parent, supervisor, small-group leader, board member, teacher, owner—then it is important to include in your prayers the people you oversee. But include also your church, your company, your city, your country. Why not all the churches? Why not pray for all believers everywhere? Why not pray for every hungry child alive?

Why not pray for "us"? For "we"? For God's will to be done?

We can only achieve our God-given potential through daily dependence on him. Prayers for "us" are more significant than prayers for "me." Reader, you matter in the surprising way God is changing the world. *You* matter, specifically. Next chapter, we're going to talk about why you matter. But we can't get to that until you understand this: We can do nothing without him, and that's where prayer comes in.

What Only God Can Do

I wish I could say that was the first time I learned this lesson. Far from it. Some things I have to keep learning over and over. I wouldn't even believe God existed if it weren't for people's prayers. For most of my life, I was an atheist. One day, while working as a pizza delivery driver, I stopped at a local bookstore to buy a copy of the Bible. It wasn't at all what I'd expected. Portions read like a fast-paced novel. To my surprise, I found the Bible believable and true. I had expected it would twist reality somewhat, softening it, sort of like *Chicken Soup for the Soul*. But the Bible is R-rated.

The God of the Bible caught me off guard. I was surprised to discover how believable he is. It seemed that if there was a god, then he would be like this God. Especially when I read about Jesus, I was awestruck. I had never read about anyone else like him. The things he said and did were so countercultural and otherworldly, I became convinced no one could have cooked this character up. He was too good for fiction. Over the coming months, people came into my life to answer questions at the right time. Articles I read or bits on the radio spoke to me at just the right moments.

Years after my baptism I began to piece together the backstory. I gradually started to remember believers God had placed in my life along the way. My best friend in junior high was a Christian. He wasn't pushy, just a great friend. I remembered teachers and neighbors who had faith for me before I had eyes to see.

I began uncovering stories of people who were praying for me. My older brother married the daughter of a missionary, and there were people in churches in South Africa and Australia praying for us. I learned about an elderly couple who lived down the street from me who prayed for my family for over twenty years before they saw, in the course of one year, my older brother baptized, and then six months later me baptized, and then six months after that my younger brother baptized.

Which all points, I believe, to the true story. Behind my story, as he is behind all the stories, was the Author and Perfecter of our faith. Only God could have orchestrated all of the dozens of people and hundreds of circumstances that he used to gradually soften and win my heart. No book, ministry, or program in all the world could have brought together the thousands of relationships and variables God used to form faith in me. There are certain things only God can do.

There's so much I don't understand about prayer. We don't know why God answers some prayers the way he does. Sometimes he seems to answer them before we even ask.[4] Sometimes it's months later.[5]

I prayed like this, for God's will to be done, for months and months, failing miserably. And then when year two started, suddenly everything was different. God's will was not for me to be comfortable. It didn't matter how much I asked him to make things better for me, it was not a prayer he was going to answer during that season of my life. He didn't rearrange the world to make it easy for me. Instead, he pulled out all the stops to make me effective at fulfilling *his* will. There can be a huge difference between God fulfilling our will and God empowering us to achieve his will.

It's not that God doesn't want things to go well for us. It's just that he also wants things to go well for those students I was teaching in Harlem. And for all my talk and posturing about being selfless and interested in serving, I wasn't. Mostly,

I just wanted a good life. I wanted to be healthy and happy, and I didn't want any hassles. But some of my students were unhealthy and unhappy and hassled continuously. Turns out God cares a lot more for them than I did, and it wasn't until I stopped praying all the woe-is-me, help-me-through-this prayers and got serious about accomplishing his will that things started to change.

And then, because God really is a good Father, it turned out pretty good for me, too. That second year was every bit as difficult as the first, but I had no idea how good things would get.

What Only You Can Do

Our Gifts Are Meant to Be Given

Out of Respect for the Dead

On the Friday before Halloween, as my kids were finishing a math problem that had something to do with least common multiples and pumpkins, I quietly lowered the blinds. When I turned out the lights, it became remarkably dark in the classroom. I wheeled my old wooden chair to the front of the room and sat down. The hinges creaked like frightened cats. All eyes were on me.

"You gonna tell us a scary story?" a girl asked.

"Well, sort of."

Kids started sliding their chairs closer, surrounding me. "Is it scary? Did somebody die?"

"Yes."

Silence.

"I need to tell you about something that happened in this school years ago, because it wouldn't be right if you didn't know. There was a math teacher here named . . . well, I should change his name. Let's call him Mr. Fitzer, out of respect for the dead."

You could hear a pin drop.

"Actually, he taught right here in this room, long before I came to this school. He was a very brilliant man, but a little strange. Sometimes, as he wrote solutions on the board, he would trail off and stare into space, just pondering mathematics. His students would look around and nudge each other, like, 'What's his deal?' Sometimes he would notice the way a leaf turned in the wind outside those windows, and it would make him stare off into space for minutes on end." I twisted and turned my hand like a leaf tumbling lazily toward the ground, staring at it for a long, thoughtful moment.

"And he was like a robot. Have any of you ever seen the old *Star Trek*?"

Hands went up.

"Well, he was like Spock. He never showed his feelings. But there was one thing he felt very strongly about. He couldn't stand it when kids didn't do their homework. His blood would boil, he'd get so mad. He developed high blood pressure and hypertension and all sorts of problems because of his bottled-up rage.

"One time, when half of the class hadn't done their homework, he trembled with fury. He stormed out of the room, out that door right into the hall. And you know what? He kicked that wall *so hard* that he broke . . . every . . . bone . . . in his foot."

Gasping. "Ew!"

"The doctors couldn't even fix it. He had to get it amputated. Do you know what that means?"

"What's 'amputated'?"

"They cut it off!" a boy answered.

"That's right . . . and they gave him a prosthetic foot, which is an artificial foot. But the ankle didn't work right, so he kind of dragged his foot and stomped when he walked. It sounded like this: *Shhh . . . thump! Shhh . . . thump! Shhh . . . thump!*

"Another time, he assigned a major report and gave them a whole week to complete it. But not one student did. Not one. He was so furious he couldn't speak. He turned as white as a ghost, and his eyes burned, and he clenched his fists and tried to shout, but . . . his heart exploded."

"Ew! Gross! What do you mean? Did it come out?"

"No, no. He had a massive heart attack and dropped dead . . . right . . . here . . . on this floor."

I pointed at the floor. They stared.

"Years later, something strange happened. A boy in the sixth grade decided it would be cute to hide in one of those closets during dismissal. While he was in there laughing to himself, they lined the kids up and marched them out. School Safety locked up the building and went home. When the boy came out an hour later, all the lights were off, and he found himself locked inside!

"He was locked in. Alone.

"He tried to use the phone, but couldn't get hold of anyone. He thought about lowering himself out of one of the windows, but it was way too far of a drop. In the end, he came back to this room to spend the night. He closed the door and pulled some chairs together for a bed, and actually managed to sleep. Until he heard the noise. He sat up with a start. The classroom was dark. The clock read midnight.

"There it was again! Off in the distance, faintly, he could hear the sound: *Shhh . . . thump! Shhh . . . thump!*"

You should have seen how wide their eyes were. I almost broke character. I literally bit the inside of my cheek to keep from smiling.

"Then he heard it much louder. It was in the hallway outside. *Shhh . . . thump! Shhh . . . thump!*

"He ran to the door and popped the latch to lock it, then closed it as quietly as he could. He could still hear it coming down the hall. *Shhh . . . thump! Shhh . . . thump!* He thought about jumping from the window but knew he'd never survive the fall, so he ran to the closet and shut himself in.

"Hiding back in the dark, all alone, he heard the sound draw closer. *Shhh . . . thump! Shhh . . . thump!* It stopped right outside that door.

"He held his breath, hoping the door was strong enough to keep out whoever—*whatever*—it was. He never heard the classroom door open, but he definitely heard the sound inside the room."

This time I made the sound by dragging my own foot across the floor and stomping it. *Shhh . . . THUMP! Shhh . . . THUMP! Shhh . . . THUMP!*

"It stopped just outside the closet door. So scared he couldn't breathe, he watched in terror as the closet doors slowly began to open. He covered his eyes with his hands and peeked through his fingers, when to his horror . . ."

At this point I jumped out of my chair toward them, waving my arms, and screamed.

You should have seen it.

Kids jumped back, sending chairs and desks scooting across the floor. Two kids actually tipped backwards and fell out of their chairs. The whole class, boys and girls alike, screamed in frequencies only dogs can hear. And their faces!

I laughed so hard. Twelve-year-olds were holding their chests and panting like they were having a heart attack, then smiling, then laughing along with me. We laughed for several minutes.

Students exclaimed, "Mr. Travis, you play too much!" and "You *scared* me!" and "Did that really happen?" Then I finished the tale.

"There was nothing there. It was just the wind. A weird vacuum from one of the windows had pulled the closet doors open, and in his fear he was imagining the sounds. It was probably just a branch hitting the side of the building somewhere. But I tell you what, from then on that kid was the first to line up at dismissal time.

"Sometimes, though, if you find yourself alone in one of these hallways, when the wind is blowing, you'll hear strange things.

"Ooo . . . orrr . . . ohme . . . errr . . .

"Ooo . . . orrr . . . ohme . . . errrk . . .

"Ooo . . . yorrr . . . ohme . . . errk.

"Dooo . . . yourrr . . . hooome . . . werrrk."

They all rolled their eyes, and I deserved it.

What Only You Can Do

I love a good story. Time off for me is time with a page-turner or a great movie. I remember campfire stories my dad told when I was in Boy Scouts. I like to tell stories, too. I'm not the best storyteller in the world, but I really enjoy it and will tell a tale when I get the chance. I had no idea how often God would use storytelling to impact these kids' lives.

Often it was just for fun, like the story I told on Halloween. Sometimes there would be a point or a lesson to it, or I'd use a story to help kids understand the potential consequences of their behavior. I even used stories to teach math. I used a story to teach the rules for multiplying and dividing signed numbers. I used a mystery story about the Unknown Number to introduce the concept of the variable in algebra.

I discovered that when I got serious about seeking God's will first and doing what I could to bring his kingdom to life on earth, he began to use interests and skills of mine in ways I wouldn't have guessed or imagined. I spent most of my own time in middle school bored, doodling and cartooning in my notebooks to pass the hours. I had no idea my fingers would remember how to draw doodles decades later, or that the characters I developed then would come in handy when a chalkboard was all I had to work with. I started an after-school art club. I started drawing custom pictures as rewards for good behavior or academic improvement, and the kids were begging for them.

Similarly, who knew that the one card trick I could perform would buy me so many points with eighth-grade gangsters in the lunchroom. I took karate for a few years in high school and remembered enough to start a karate club after school.

It was even more thrilling to discover God redeeming parts of my life I had always regarded as a mistake. For example, I entered college as a computer engineering major because I had always done okay at math and science, and I really didn't know what else to do. I endured that major until the day I looked around my C++ programming class and realized everyone else was actually interested in this stuff. Within a week, I switched my major to English literature and never looked back. That is, until I felt like God was calling me to make a difference in NYC public schools and discovered they needed math teachers. Those calculus credits I'd accumulated way back then qualified me for the job.

I think most of us have had experiences like that. We've made bad decisions or come to tough spots in life when we had to backtrack and take the other fork in the road. Some of our greatest regrets and sources of pain come from seasons in our lives like these. The unfinished degree, the failed business, or the girl who got away can haunt us for the rest of our lives. Many people live trapped in the cage of what-might-have-been.

Friends, bad things happen to us for all kinds of reasons. Often it's our own stupid fault (speaking for myself). Sometimes we get pinched for doing the right thing. In the book of Job, the Bible teaches that it's beyond us to really understand why these things happen. We can't know all the whys, but we can know this: God is good, he loves us, "And we know that in all things God works for the good of those who love him, who have been called according to his purpose."[1] I'm discovering God uses it all, even our own bone-headed choices. He shapes our character and gives us compassion and grace for others. And we learn things along the way that God will use to advance his purposes and his kingdom.

In addition to your experiences, God will use who you are. He made you for a reason. Your personality, skills, strengths, and gifts are there for a purpose. God has entrusted you, and not another, with a specific mix of gifts and talents.

"We have different gifts, according to the grace given to each of us."[2] God has given us power over our own selves, and if we do not use our gifts for his glory, then no one will use them for us.

Gifts Are Meant to Be Given

Jesus told this story about the kingdom of heaven:

> It will be like a man going on a journey, who called his servants and entrusted his wealth to them. To one he gave five bags of gold, to another two bags, and to another one bag, each according to his ability. Then he went on his journey. The man who had received five bags of gold went at once and put his money to work and gained five bags more. So also, the one with two bags of gold gained two more. But the man who had received one bag went off, dug a hole in the ground and hid his master's money.[3]

In older versions of the Bible, "bags of gold" is translated as "talents," which was the name of a very valuable coin. "Bags of gold" is a better way for us to understand the value. But I miss the serendipitous double meaning of the word "talent" in English, because I think this story isn't only talking about the wealth God entrusts to us, but also our gifts, our abilities, our "talents."

At this point in the story, I imagine people listening to Jesus wondered what would happen. What the third servant did sounds pretty reasonable. The master "entrusted his wealth" to him. Hiding it and keeping it safe sounds like a responsible thing to do. The other two servants risked it on the market and were lucky enough to turn a profit. But what if they hadn't? What if they'd lost it all? Imagine how angry the master would be to return home to discover the loss.

> After a long time the master of those servants returned and settled accounts with them. The man who had received five bags of gold brought the other five. "Master," he said, "you entrusted me with five bags of gold. See, I have gained five more."
>
> His master replied, "Well done, good and faithful servant! You have been faithful with a few things; I will put you in charge of many things. Come and share your master's happiness!"
>
> The man with two bags of gold also came. "Master," he said, "you entrusted me with two bags of gold; see, I have gained two more."
>
> His master replied, "Well done, good and faithful servant! You have been faithful with a few things; I will put you in charge of many things. Come and share your master's happiness!"[4]

Pay careful attention to the master's words. He did not say, "Well done! You made me so much richer!" He did not say, "Well done! You succeeded in the marketplace!" The master said, "Well done, good and *faithful* servant! You have been *faithful*" (emphasis mine). The word translated here as "faithful" is the Greek word *pistos*. *Pistos* is most often translated as faithful, but it's more than just what we think of as "faithful." It is a rich word sometimes translated as trustworthy, sure, believing, and true, depending on the context. When Thomas stood face-to-face with the impossible, Jesus back from the grave days after being murdered and buried, it was too much for him to believe. But Jesus said, "Put your finger here; see my hands. Reach out your hand and put it into my side. Stop doubting and believe."⁵ Jesus said to Thomas, "Stop doubting and *pistos.*" Don't be faithless, but faithful. When 1 Timothy 4:10 says, "That is why we labor and strive, because we have put our hope in the living God, who is the Savior of all people, and especially of those who believe," it says, ". . . and especially those who *pistos.*"

Getting back to the story at hand, the master said, "Well done! You have been faithful, true, trustworthy, believing. You have been full of faith." The master was pleased because the servants had done what he had asked them to do. He entrusted his wealth to them in order for them to use it. These first two servants had the faith to take the risk.

I imagine the third servant was growing anxious at this point. Hiding the treasure to keep it safe might have been prudent or responsible, but it wasn't faithful. He marshaled his defense and tried to justify himself.

"Master," he said, "I knew that you are a hard man, harvesting where you have not sown and gathering where you have not scattered seed. So I was afraid and went out and hid your gold in the ground. See, here is what belongs to you."

His master replied, "You wicked, lazy servant! So you knew that I harvest where I have not sown and gather where I have not scattered seed? Well then, you should have put my money on deposit with the bankers, so that when I returned I would have received it back with interest.

"So take the bag of gold from him and give it to the one who has ten bags. For whoever has will be given more, and they will have an abundance. Whoever does not have, even what they have will be taken from them. And throw that worthless servant outside, into the darkness, where there will be weeping and gnashing of teeth."[6]

The third servant tried to blame his own faithlessness and laziness on his master. He said the master was a "hard man" and an unjust man, harvesting crops he hadn't planted—in other words, taking what he hadn't earned for himself. What a terrifying thing to believe about your master. And as this servant believed, so was his master revealed to him. When Jesus told a very similar story in Luke, the master replied to the wicked servant by saying, "I will judge you by your own words, you wicked servant!"[7]

I wish this story had a couple of other characters in it. I wish there was another servant who invested the master's wealth faithfully but lost it all spectacularly. I suspect the master would have said, "Well done, good and *faithful* servant." I wish there was yet another servant who was lazy and chickened out and hid the money, but chose to own up to it faithfully. "Master, I was lazy and self-centered, so I buried what you gave me. I'm so sorry. I should have been faithful." I like to think the master might have said, "Now that you are faithful, I will trust you again."

Jesus did not include those other servants in the story. But he did teach a critical lesson about all God has entrusted to us. It is this: Our gifts are meant to be given. "For whoever has will be given more, and they will have an abundance."[8]

I thought I understood mathematics, thought I *had* math, so to speak, until I tried to teach it to middle school students. I quickly realized I didn't have as much math as I thought I did. But as I used it, taught it, gave it away, my hold on math firmed up. I used to tell my students, "You don't understand something until you can make someone else understand it." This is a law of reality. Our gifts are meant to be given.

The Lord wants us to use the gifts he's given us for others. If we don't, even the gifts we have will be taken from us. He doesn't give them for us to keep, but if we give them, then we truly own them, and he will give us more. I think God would like to give us more than we ever dare to dream. He just needs to know we'll use what he gives us in the way he would use it. If we're just going to take his gifts and sit on them, or use them only to benefit ourselves, or wield them recklessly and tear up the place, he's going to take them away.

One of my favorite verses in all the Bible—one that I find myself constantly thinking about, teaching about, writing about, is 1 Peter 4:10: "Each of you should use whatever gift you have received to serve others, as faithful stewards of God's grace in its various forms."

Like Lightning Striking Eternity

Much has been made about the different kinds of spiritual gifts and the need to understand our giftedness and serve in areas where we're gifted. It is true, but it isn't the whole truth. The Bible certainly teaches that God creates each person to be unique, and he gives all followers of Jesus important spiritual gifts. We must grow to understand ourselves and how best to utilize our gifts for his purposes. But I don't think it's as simple as we sometimes think. I'm not certain there is a clearly defined list of spiritual gifts in Scripture that God chooses from for each person. Look at Romans 12:3–8, 1 Corinthians 12:7–10, Ephesians 4:11, and 1 Peter 4:10–11, and you will find very different lists of very different gifts and roles. But there is one overarching theme: Everyone is gifted somehow for the benefit of others. "Now to each one the manifestation of the Spirit is given for the common good."[9]

We can be tempted to worry about which gifts we have or should have or how they work and miss the main point, which is that gifts are meant to be given. They are meant to be used. And as you use your gifts for God's purposes, you'll grow to understand your giftedness better, and he'll trust you with more. If you wait to understand your gifts before using them, you might find at the end of your days that you've buried them and have some explaining to do.

Short version: Get involved. Start serving. Start using whatever you have to do whatever you can for him.

If you don't, you'll be passed by. God will find another way to accomplish his will, no worries there. But there is no one who can give your gifts but you. And in the end, the only thing that will matter to us is what the master has to say. Which gifts we had won't matter. The only thing that will matter is what we did with what we had. Only our *pistos*, our faithfulness, counts. Whether your gifts are the sort people respect or the kind people ignore, there is One watching who doesn't miss a thing.

There is a massive reversal of significance coming. All of the things we think matter so much—success, being noticed, even making a difference—are all so temporary and short-sighted. Meanwhile, the One this world ignores, the gentle God who put himself last for us, he is all that will matter. No amount of hardship, sacrifice, or patient waiting will seem too high a price to pay for the privilege of hearing the One who matters say with a smile, "Well done, good and faithful servant! You have been faithful with a few things; I will put you in charge of many things. Come and share your master's happiness!"

Sometimes you hear people say things like, "You've got to believe in yourself," but that's nonsense. We doubt our own potential not because we fail to believe in ourselves, but because we fail to believe in God. God says he will conform us into the image of Christ. Do you believe he will do what he says? Don't waste your time trying to believe in yourself. Believe in God. "For we are God's handiwork, created in Christ Jesus to do good works, which God prepared in advance for us to do."[10]

In the surprising way that God is changing the world, you matter more than you imagine. You needn't be perfect, so do not shrink back. Until you accomplish it, you are invincible. Neither heaven nor earth, nor powers nor accidents, can take you from this world until God calls you home. And if you even attempt to use your gifts for others, the Mighty God of heaven and Earth will strengthen you. "For the eyes of the LORD range throughout the earth to strengthen those whose hearts are fully committed to him."[11] He will dispatch beautiful and terrible warrior angels to uphold your cause. He will reach from heaven and bend the fabric of the universe to assist you. He will stand beside you himself, take your hand, give you his ear, and be like a friend and a partner to you. His Spirit will flow from your heart according to his purposes.[12]

If you dip even just the tip of your toe in his will, it will refresh your soul with a surge of purpose. If you can catch even just the echo of an echo of it, your soul will dance to the song of significance. If you take hold of it, everything that matters will matter more than anything has ever mattered to you before. Your days will leap forth like lightning striking eternity.

Reader, I'd like to let you in on something that is missing from the world. We are missing all that God will do through you.

Whatever You Do

Any Moment Can Matter

This Strange Detachment

It was thrilling to help bring a little order into such a chaotic, dysfunctional environment. Over time, as God did all the things only he can do and worked through me in ways I'd never imagined, I began to see a small pocket of his kingdom forming in room 319. Occasionally someone would ask how I kept my peace in such a nightmare, and I would explain, "I've got my own little kingdom going on in that room. I can't change the big picture, but the little piece I'm in charge of is different." I preached at my students all the time: "I don't care how it works on the street or in the halls, I'm tellin' you how it works in Mr. Travis's classroom." I had two classroom rules. Number one: Anything that disrupts learning or teaching is a problem. Number two: Treat others the way you want to be treated.

Of course, I didn't exactly come up with that second one on my own.[1] But that's just the point. I wasn't really carving out my own kingdom at all. I was partnered with Jesus to bring his kingdom to earth. That's a very important distinction, because advancing his kingdom is much bigger and more important than anything I could do for myself in a failing inner-city middle school no one had ever heard of. The richest and most powerful people alive cannot carve out anything for themselves more significant than the kingdom of heaven.

Gradually I developed this strange detachment from my work, which was freeing, even exhilarating. I simultaneously worked harder and felt less stressed. It wasn't about me. My work, my efforts, and even my life weren't the focus anymore. I often had to sacrifice for the cause. I had to stay late and love people who were difficult to love. Partnering with Jesus to advance his kingdom is often difficult and unpleasant, but there are some unexpected upsides. It is never boring. In fact, it's the adventure of a lifetime. Along the way, God creates moments that are magical because they matter.

He Said We Are More Valuable

As I attempted to look at my days from God's perspective, I noticed important moments happening more often. During seasons when I am self-focused, most days just run together. On the days when I manage to be God-focused, I regularly experience significant events. Here are four that occurred in a single day in the life of a middle-school math teacher.

One

A friend asked me to officiate at his wedding, so I requested a personal day off work to do it. I explained to my class that I was going to be absent and lectured them about how they represent me when I'm gone and how much that matters to me. I used my best lecture voice, a special tone I cultivated that made it clear I would gladly go on lecturing well into their lunch period if I felt they weren't paying attention. "Any questions, concerns, comments?" I asked.[2]

"What are you doin'?"

"I'm going to a wedding."

Now, to understand what happened next, you need to know the following: Phillip was a very small, consistently hilarious troublemaker who once saw a photo of my wife in my phone and fell instantly in love with her. The moment the words "I'm going to a wedding" left my mouth, Phillip shot out of his chair and shouted, "Can I have your ex-wife?!"

I laughed so hard I cried. My students had never seen me laugh that hard. My girls were giggling and calling out, "He *cryin'*! He *cryin'*!"

Wiping my eyes, I tried to clarify. "No, no, no . . . I'm *officiating* at this wedding. Do you know what that means?"

"You the best man?"

"Nope, it means I'm the one who leads them to take their vows."

Blank stares.

"It means I'm the pastor."

"Oh! You the one who says, 'You may now kiss the bride'?"

"Yes."

That was a big hit with the girls.

Two

Not one hour later, I was in the stairwell taking a class to the cafeteria, waiting for them to straighten up their lines. A kid from another class who was generally disrespectful and usually up to no good pushed through me to get downstairs, apparently frustrated with the holdup.

A few minutes later I found him in the cafeteria and knelt beside him. He turned away, but I knew he was listening. More important, his friends were listening. I had a reputation to maintain if I ever wanted to get anything done. That was a necessary part of this job I didn't particularly care for, but let one rumor get out about a teacher being "soft," and your class is out of control and kids get hurt.

"You're an idiot," I said flatly.

He sucked his teeth.

"I don't care what anyone says, you are what you do. You aren't big enough to hurt me, but I can get you suspended for what you did. I won't, because I care about you more than you do. But if you don't smarten up, you might as well just push yourself around."

Three

After lunch that same day, a new student was making sexual jokes with one of my girls. I had already pegged him as a sexual predator, having caught him touching other boys and girls inappropriately. He was one of many students discharged from charter schools only to land with us, the bottom of the public school barrel. It was always such a tender balance, trying to help bullies and predators but also protecting the rest of the class. I learned to squash dangerous students as fast as I could or else many others would get hurt in the long run.

I was solving a problem on the board when I heard him inviting one of my girls to do something kids that age shouldn't even know the meaning of. I bristled. I thought, *Should I deal with this right now?*

But the words were already leaving my mouth. "You know what?" I set the marker down and turned away from the board. "Let me just deal with this right now."

I wish you could know how out of character this sort of thing was for me. Part of why I was so ineffective the first year was that I was too soft by nature. I thought I was being nice when really I was being a coward and cruel to those I failed to protect. But God had taught me along the way and provided power I didn't have.

I mustered all the volume I could. I dug deep, forcing the words out from my diaphragm. I pointed. I accented my main points by clapping as loudly as I could.

"That doesn't happen here. I swear if you make me stop class to deal with your nastiness one more time, I'm gonna find a way to make you pay."

The class was silent. I was four feet from this kid, going off (or as they say in Harlem, going "in").

"You all know I'm fair, right?" I looked around the room and kids actually nodded. "I don't use the dean. . . . I handle my own business right here. But, kid, I swear I'm gonna find a way to deal with you that you will *not* like.

"This space is pure. When you cross that door right there, you are in a pure place, and I don't care how you feel about that. You wanna be all sneaky, but I'm gonna blow your spot up. Now, this is the second time I've stopped instruction to straighten you out. There won't be a third. So tell me right now, are you finished? If you're not, then man up and let's deal with it right now. Don't say you're done and then wait till I turn my back, because I swear I'm gonna make you regret it. So, are you done?"

And I waited. I waited until he nodded and looked down.

I know they teach you in education programs not to use shame or disrespect a kid in front of his peers. And I agree, it's a nasty way to get things done. A wiser man might have found a better way. But his victims, and the victims of other bullies and predators, were always appreciative to have this little moment in their day, a couple of periods in math class, where the world worked just a little bit as it should. And by the end of the year, I had won him over a little, too. We joked around regularly, and he joined my karate club.

Four

Finally, at the end of that same day, we had an assembly for a talent show, and a couple of our students performed. One of the girls sang "His Eye Is on the Sparrow." It was beautiful. The boys sitting near me had been singing along with a Mary J. Blige song right before it, but now they stopped. One of them said, "I don't know this song."

I said, "You want to know where it comes from?"

"Yeah."

"In the Bible Jesus said that a sparrow doesn't fall to the ground without God knowing about it." I waited for a moment for that to sink in and added, "Then he said we are more valuable to God than many sparrows."

They were quiet for a few moments. Then one of them smiled and said, "That's tough!"

I chuckled and said, "Yeah, it is, isn't it?"

I had dozens of days like that one. They weren't all chock-full of dramatic moments, but every day that I focused on God's will and his kingdom first, and not my own, was meaningful. This is not an easy path to walk. It is very difficult, and it is narrow. I feel like I keep slipping off and finding my way back on.

It costs something, but it is significant.

And Still Be at Peace

The irony of it all still tickles me today. What could possibly be more *insignificant* than a guy who teaches math to middle-schoolers at a school where the vast majority of the students will fail the state exams, and statistically, over half will drop out of school before they graduate high school? Yet it was the most significant year of my life.

It was significant only because I was doing it for him. The Bible says, "Whatever you do, work at it with all your heart, as working for the Lord, not for human masters, since you know that you will receive an inheritance from the Lord as a reward. It is the Lord Christ you are serving."[3] Whatever you do—your job, looking for a job, raising your kids, finishing school—whatever you do, work at it with all your heart.

Remember that God put himself last for us because he wants our love and our hearts. Whatever you do, work at it as if you're working for the Lord, because you know his reward is a sure thing, and it is Jesus you are truly serving. I can tell you from personal experience that when you're working for the Lord, you can lay your head on your pillow at night feeling great about what you've accomplished, no matter what results your efforts seem to have. You can get through days when it seems like not one student has learned a single thing, when in fact they forgot things you thought they knew, and then you make a bunch of management blunders that lead to nasty fights, and then spend two solid hours scrubbing obscene graffiti and scraping chewing gum. You can do that and still be at peace, knowing you did what was asked of you.

You can keep changing diapers and reading the same picture books over and over again. You can do all the tedious paper work. You can pick up her slack even though you know she will never thank you for it. You can make your boss look good even though he's incompetent. You can do all this and know that there is a sure reward, and that it matters, because you aren't working for him or her or them. "It is the Lord Christ you are serving."[4]

Jesus was a carpenter. This simple fact has been repeated so many times that we've lost all sensitivity to it. But now that I'm a pastor and a writer, I've noticed people put a little more weight on my words than they did when I was a middle-school math teacher. Would we pay attention to what a carpenter had to say about God? I know I am as guilty of this as anyone. Give me the conference speaker, the pastor of the big church, the person being interviewed on TV—they've got something important to say. Jesus' contemporaries had the same view of significance we do. When Jesus came to teach in his hometown where everyone knew who he was and how he put food on the table, "they were amazed," it says in the Scripture. "Where did this man get this wisdom and these miraculous powers?" they asked. "Isn't this the carpenter's son?"[5]

It was the same with Jesus' first followers. These ordinary men, because they had been with Jesus, astonished others with their understanding and power. When the Sanhedrin—the highest council of priests and the most influential, educated, and powerful religious leaders in Israel—heard Peter and John talk about Jesus, they were "astonished." The Bible says, "When they saw the courage of Peter and John and realized that they were unschooled, ordinary men, they were astonished and they took note that these men had been with Jesus."[6] They recognized there was something very significant about them and took note that they "had been with Jesus." Paul, likewise, while a tireless church planter, courageous missionary, and author of much of the New Testament, didn't make his money that way. He was a tentmaker.[7]

I can't shake the feeling that we have associated people's professions with how significant they are to God's work in a way the Bible does not. According to the Bible, every believer is a priest to the world.[8] And you cannot read the Scriptures without noticing that our work matters to God. When it came time to build the temple, God inspired metalworkers, embroiderers, and craftsmen of all sorts to advance his kingdom purposes.[9] I do not think my work as a church planter and a writer is even a tiny bit more significant than my work as a math teacher was. The only thing that makes my work matter is doing it for the Lord. Nothing else matters at all.

Sometimes I'll hear pastors and other religious types issue challenges for people to leave their careers and "enter the ministry" or "go on the mission field." Please don't hear me wrong. We desperately need people to work at churches and nonprofits and go overseas to spread the gospel. There are a whole lot of people ignoring this call, and the kingdom suffers for it. That said, sometimes hearing challenges like that is heartrending for me because what we need even more than people in paid ministry is for people to *be* ministers, whatever they do. We need people who recognize their jobs and their neighborhoods as mission fields, and work to bring God's kingdom to earth in their own circles of influence.

If you have ever been made to feel your work is not a ministry, it's time to erase that memory from your mind. We need more teachers and more people in finance and more caregivers. In the same way God calls people to work in churches and through missions organizations, God is calling others to be ministers where they are, in the marketplace or at home. The challenge for most of us isn't to change the work we do but to change who we're doing it for.

Get serious about a daily surrender to God, and the big picture works itself out. I was on staff at a church for years. Then I taught math at an inner-city school. Now I'm part of a team planting a church in Manhattan. Who knows what comes next? I pray God will keep me soft and teachable to follow him wherever that leads. But whatever he would have me do, it must be for him.

There Is Something Substantial About Them

I'm not talking about working harder, though that could be part of it. But the shift is more fundamental than that.

Jesus is not calling you to give more of yourself to God.

Jesus is calling you to give everything to him.

The blessed irony is that he knows what's good for us better than we do. If we do give everything to him, many of us will suffer. Almost all will be disciplined from time to time. Nevertheless, many of us will find ourselves resting more, spending more time with loved ones, enjoying our lives, and still getting more accomplished than we ever have before.[10]

Jesus said it like this: "If you cling to your life, you will lose it, and if you let your life go, you will save it."[11] We must take this tendency to be our own god by the scruff of the neck, drag it to the door, and give it a good kick in the pants to help it on its way. We must starve it and neglect it and ignore it. And when it comes back tomorrow, as it will, then we must once again take it by the scruff of the neck and do it all over again. If we try to hold on to our lives, working harder to fit more God stuff into them, we'll be miserable and ineffective.

When you meet people who get this, people who have re-ordered their lives to seek God's kingdom first and to love their neighbors as themselves, there is something substantial about them. What they do to earn their living may or may not be significant in the eyes of the world, but there's something unusual about the effect they have on the world.

Alicia Hansen is a professional photographer who has worked in the industry for close to two decades with major media sources like *National Geographic*. Her demeanor seems shy and unassuming, almost timid. Meeting her, it might be very easy to miss the significance of her life, or the courage she shows by getting deeply involved in the lives of inner-city students.

Years ago she responded to the presence of kids in her neighborhood by forming an organization called NYC Salt. She invited eighth-graders to learn photography from her and other professionals she brings to help. Over the years, the students' competence with photography grew. Their work is incredible. Along the way they received all kinds of mentoring and have been networked with decision-makers. NYC Salt recently graduated its first group of high-school seniors. Seven out of the eight went to college. The eighth will soon. They are mostly majoring in fine arts or photography, and three of them received full-ride scholarships.

They are all the first in their families to go to college.

According to Alicia, it's been a long, difficult, sometimes messy road. Helping eight students pick schools, apply, write entrance essays, and make deadlines for financial aid forms is not very glamorous work. She flew to their universities to help settle the students in. She took them to the store to buy sheets for their dorm-room beds. NYC Salt now has eighteen new students in the program and a waiting list of those who would like to be. Alicia is not paid for this. The board of NYC Salt would like to change that in the future, to free her up to focus on work with the students more, because there is no shortage of students who would benefit from this. But right now her work with NYC Salt is pro bono.[12]

Alicia is a professional photographer. She is a minister.

In 1986 a hospice volunteer named Ganga Stone visited a terminal AIDS patient named Richard Sayles. On that fateful day, Stone discovered her patient was too ill to prepare food for himself, so she cooked a meal for him and brought it along on her next visit. One meal seems so insignificant, but it brought a little hope to a desperate situation. Try to remember what a bowl of chicken soup from your mom did for you when you were sick. In those days, AIDS was very misunderstood. Terminal patients were released from hospitals to die alone, often ostracized by neighbors and family.

Stone realized her patient had specific nutritional needs, so she researched his condition and prepared a meal tailored to those needs. On her way to deliver it, a minister she knew from the neighborhood asked her what she was doing. When she explained, he replied, "You're not just delivering food . . . you're delivering God's love."[13] Ganga Stone realized at that moment the name for this new effort.

I doubt she had any idea that God's Love We Deliver would grow over the next two years to provide fifty nutritional meals daily from a kitchen on the Upper West Side of New York City, expand to include people who suffer from other terminal diseases like cancer and Alzheimer's, and then grow from there to deliver a total of 12 million meals (so far) at a rate of four thousand per weekday.

God's Love We Deliver started with some simple ideas. First, they would never keep a waiting list, always finding a way to respond with meals within twenty-four hours for people in these desperate situations. Second, they would never charge for a meal, regardless of the patient's income level. Ganga Stone was only the first volunteer with God's Love We Deliver. Today, 7,600 people volunteer each year, peeling carrots, cooking rice, loading vans, placing bags of good food in sick people's hands, and giving hugs.

Ganga Stone was a hospice volunteer. She is a minister.

But How We Will Emerge

What if we all truly sought God's kingdom first? What if every Christian alive embraced his or her destiny to bring God's kingdom to earth? Through daily surrender and working at whatever we do with all our hearts, we could change everything. If the church roused herself and wiped the sleep from her eyes and started serving the Lord every day, I don't think the world would know what to do with her.

A friend of mine, Aaron Brockett, who leads a church in Indianapolis, cast a compelling vision for participants in his church. As part of a series of messages about how to be a Christ-follower in the workplace, he described an imaginary meeting of all the bosses of all "the businesses, organizations, hospitals, offices, and stores" to compare notes about their best employees. Aaron dreamed about all these supervisors discovering that all their best employees were a part of the church.[14]

I heard another pastor say recently that if just one family from every church in the state of Ohio adopted just one foster care kid, then Ohio would no longer need a foster care system.[15]

What if we could eradicate sexual slavery in the entire world? Why can't we?

I had such a difficult time writing this book precisely because I had been meditating so much on significance. The Bible says, "Of making many books there is no end."[16] Like all the other books, this one is utterly doomed to oblivion. The pages will dry-rot. The words will be utterly forgotten. Whether one person reads it or a million, the book itself is insignificant. It really won't take long for us to forget all about it. In the scope of human history, a hundred years are a blink. To the eternal God, a billion years are a flickering shadow.

God's kingdom is all that matters. Love for God and love for others. If just one person who reads this book redirects the trajectory of his or her life to accomplish God's will instead of his or her own, then this book will have been significant. When this world roasts in the purifying fires of judgment, not one single human achievement will endure.

Not a deed. Not a word. Nothing.

The mountains, monuments, systems, structures, even the very ideas of them will crumble and disintegrate. Only love for the eternal One will endure. Only our souls and the souls of others. Only what we've done for God and for others will matter.

But we will emerge from the wreckage like butterflies struggling from the dead husk. We think this world is where the action is, and the next world doesn't matter. We tend to think that when it's all gone—when all the celebrity, money, sex, power, and success are gone—what's left will be small and boring. How little faith we have! How foolish!

Lying in wait within all this insignificance is your real self, your soul, the "you" God meant when he spoke your name and you sprang out of the biological, temporal mess. By God, you will rise forth from the wreckage, shining with the Light of Ages. You will stretch your wings across galaxies and take long strides over millennia and wield your spiritual gifts in the power of his Spirit. He will make you a Christian, a little Christ, so much like your big brother, righteous and pure and loved by God, a great pleasure to him. The very source of existence will beam with pride when he beholds what he accomplished in you.

God will conform you to his image. If you follow him, you cannot help it. It is your destiny, and by him, you'll get there. No more downcast eyes. Lift your wretched spirit and take hold of the fact that it is the poor in spirit who are blessed. Lift your doubtful heart and believe. Lift your ordinary days to forever. Lift your eyes to the only Being worthy of the glory of your life.

When God made you, he had an idea. When Christ came into your life, he put you on the path. What will you do now? What God-dreams rise from within? What can you do with this life that matters? Be a priest for all those sheep God has placed in your path and intercede for them. Take your talent and invest it.

You are not just a mom. You are not just an employee. You are not just a student, friend, grandfather, neighbor, or whatever silly little thing you think you are or they labeled you or that the media says you are. In the eyes of the world, you may never matter much. If you matter at all, you won't for long. Give it a hundred years and almost all of us will be forgotten. Give it ten thousand years for the rest.

But, reader, in the surprising way God is changing the world, you matter.

You matter.

You matter.

Welcome Forever

Generosity Is a Call Not to Miss Out

The Lying Cheat

Jesus told some weird stories.

He must have been so interesting to listen to because he used passionate, imaginative language. He talked about Paradise in ways that made hearts ache. His words about judgment can feel like a cold slap in the face. And he told stories that are borderline irreverent. In one, Jesus compared God to a cantankerous neighbor who wouldn't want to get out of bed for a friend in need.[1] In another, God was like an unjust judge who wouldn't help a desperate widow.[2]

The "good guys" in Jesus' stories were often just as surprising. The despised Samaritan—not the priest or religious leader—was the good neighbor to the man who fell victim to robbers. We often miss the impact of this. To get the same kind of emotional reaction in today's churches that Jesus got from his audience, he would have to tell the story of "The Good Muslim," or maybe "The Good Child Molester."

One time, Jesus said to the religious authorities, "Truly I tell you, the tax collectors and the prostitutes are entering the kingdom of God ahead of you."[3] Because they repented and believed, the men who extorted money from innocent people and the women who had sex for money were ahead of the preachers and seminarians in the line for heaven. I write that as a preacher and a seminarian who needs to be reminded of it. Jesus' teaching was infuriating to self-righteous people and refreshing to sinners.

Jesus told a weird story like that in Luke 16:1–7:

> There was a rich man whose manager was accused of wasting his possessions. So he called him in and asked him, "What is this I hear about you? Give an account of your management, because you cannot be manager any longer."
>
> The manager said to himself, "What shall I do now? My master is taking away my job. I'm not strong enough to dig, and I'm ashamed to beg—I know what I'll do so that, when I lose my job here, people will welcome me into their houses."
>
> So he called in each one of his master's debtors. He asked the first, "How much do you owe my master?"
>
> "Nine hundred gallons of olive oil," he replied.
>
> The manager told him, "Take your bill, sit down quickly, and make it four hundred and fifty."
>
> Then he asked the second, "And how much do you owe?"
>
> "A thousand bushels of wheat," he replied.
>
> He told him, "Take your bill and make it eight hundred."

Now, just to make sure we're tracking with the story to this point, I want to be clear. This manager was going to get fired, so in order to make friends, he falsified documents and committed fraud. Imagine these meetings he had with the debtors. It would be as if someone from the bank who held your car note called and said, "Hey, you know how you owe us a bunch of money? Well, we'd like to cut the amount you owe in half. No, that's right! I know, I know, it is unusual, isn't it? But you can breathe a sigh of relief. You owe us less than you thought. I tell you what, why don't you go ahead and quickly pay the balance so I can get you the title—you know, just in case the company changes its mind. Oh yeah, and by the way, is there any chance I can crash with you next week?"

As in many of Jesus' stories, the God-character does not react how we might expect. "The master commended the dishonest manager because he had acted shrewdly. For the people of this world are more shrewd in dealing with their own kind than are the people of the light."[4]

What? The master *commends* the *dishonest* manager? In most Bibles, the subtitle for this parable is something like "The Shrewd Manager." It should read "The Lying Cheat." This man had been accused of wasting the master's possessions, and then quickly went on a debt-slashing rampage before security could escort him from the building with his box full of personal effects. And the master commends him for it.

Unlike some of Jesus' more mysterious teachings, we do not need to guess about the meaning of this story. Jesus explains it. "I tell you, use worldly wealth to gain friends for yourselves, so that when it is gone, you will be welcomed into eternal dwellings."[5]

Use worldly wealth to gain forever friends. Possessions wear out, but people last forever. Use things that do not last forever to affect things that do.

There Is an Antidote

Have you ever thought about the possessions that really matter to people? Lindsay and I have a set of old cloth napkins we could easily replace at the thrift store if we wanted to, except that they were her Granny's, who has gone on to be with the Lord, so they can never be replaced. I hang on to a pocketknife my older brother gave me before he moved to Australia. These things aren't valuable by any objective standard, but they are worth a lot to us.

My mother has a watercolor painting I made for her in seventh grade hanging on a wall in her house to this day, and trust me, it's not a very good painting. You might own books you'll never read again, or clothes you'll never wear, because they were gifts. Some heirlooms are valuable, but others aren't, except that they are heirlooms. Your engagement ring is worth more to you than another more expensive ring. A crayon drawing gets a prominent place on the fridge. An absolutely hideous tie is suddenly worth wearing out in public when it's a Father's Day gift from a six-year-old.

In my little section of shelf at our church office, I have one of my most prized possessions. It is a particle-board plaque with a sticker on it, an award that you could probably order online for $5.99. It looks cheesy. The sticker reads "Teacher of the Year. Christopher Travis." This award is almost a joke because of how insignificant it is to have been named Teacher of the Year at one of the thousands of schools in one of the thousands of school districts in our country. The school doesn't even exist anymore. It was so bad they shut it down. But to me it represents the names and faces of dozens of students I loved dearly, in word and deed, and so it matters.

Our hearts know people are more important than things are, that's why we value these silly items. They symbolize a relationship, so they matter. They wouldn't have mattered at all if it weren't for the people who owned them or gave them or made them. And they probably wouldn't matter much to anyone who didn't know where they came from. But if your house were on fire and as you rushed out you only had time to snatch a couple of things from the flames, I bet you'd go for the photographs, the scrapbook, or the handwritten letters from your significant other. You'd go for the things that captured memories of people. Our hearts know this well because our hearts understand that relationships are more important than anything else.

Our hearts know this, but we are conflicted.

It sneaks in a hundred different ways. We start to think money will mean freedom for us, to not have to work, to travel wherever we want, to do whatever we want. We think it will mean happiness. We think it'll mean significance. Sometimes I get to hang out with rich people. Trust me, the things that make a rich man's life matter are the very same things that make a poor man's life matter: his relationship with God and with others.

It also sneaks in through fear. What if I lose my job? What if the market goes sour again? Don't get me wrong, there's nothing inherently wrong with money. Money can be used for God's purposes and for relationships. Money we spend on ourselves can be necessary, fun, even important. It is seldom meaningful, though. Instead of mastering money and using it to serve God, how many of us are serving money instead?

Psalm 106:10 says, "They traded their glorious God for a statue of a grass-eating bull" (NLT). This verse is talking about the time the Israelites forsook God, who rescued them from brutal slavery in Egypt, and instead worshiped a statue of a calf they made from gold with their own hands. Does anyone else find it ironic that the icon of Wall Street, the financial capital of the world, is a bronze-colored bull? Again, please don't hear me wrong. I am not saying you cannot work in finance and follow God. On the contrary, we desperately need more people in the money industry who are serving God instead of money.

Jesus concluded the story of this dishonest manager with these words:

> Whoever can be trusted with very little can also be trusted with much, and whoever is dishonest with very little will also be dishonest with much. So if you have not been trustworthy in handling worldly wealth, who will trust you with true riches? And if you have not been trustworthy with someone else's property, who will give you property of your own?
>
> No one can serve two masters. Either you will hate the one and love the other, or you will be devoted to the one and despise the other. You cannot serve both God and money.[6]

Talk about a Scripture we desperately want to explain away. We want to say, *Sure I can! I can love God and money, no problem.* But Jesus says we're fooling ourselves.

That always makes us feel uncomfortable, and it makes some people furious. It did in Jesus' day, too. "The Pharisees, who loved money, heard all this and were sneering at Jesus. He said to them, 'You are the ones who justify yourselves in the eyes of others, but God knows your hearts. What people value highly is detestable in God's sight.'"[7]

That is very strong language, and we ignore it at our own peril. Serving money is spiritually deadly because it damages our relationship with God. Jesus says we cannot serve both God and money. Loving money is the root of all kinds of evil.[8] It is a deadly poison.

But there is an antidote.

It Broke the Illusion

There is a tantalizing promise in that passage of Scripture. Jesus asked, "If you have not been trustworthy in handling worldly wealth, who will trust you with true riches?"[9]

True riches. What could they be?

During my second year teaching, Silly Bandz became very popular. If you haven't interacted with children in a while, Silly Bandz are colored rubber bands made in the shapes of animals and musical instruments and all sorts of other things. Who knows why certain things catch on, but for a couple of years, Silly Bandz were the new, hot thing. Six-foot gangsters wanted them. No kidding. This was great for teachers because they were inexpensive and made great incentives. One day I was organizing some things in my desk and I needed a rubber band for a stack of index cards. Several of the boys in my class were nearby, so I asked them, "Who wants to give me a Silly Bandz?"

"What for?"

"I just need one. Come on, someone help me out." It was funny to watch their faces, because these things had taken on real value in the kid economy. In addition to being a fun toy, they had become a currency in the middle school marketplace. It was as if I'd just asked, "Can someone give me twenty bucks, just 'cause?" I could tell a couple of them wanted to, but they were struggling.

"What'chu gonna give for it?"

I had already decided what I was going to do, but concealed it as, "You will get the satisfaction of knowing you did something nice for a teacher who has been good to you."

After a long moment of consideration, one of them plucked out a red dinosaur-shaped Silly Bandz and handed it over. "Thanks, man. Here." I gave him a dollar. With a dollar he could go buy a dozen Silly Bandz at the corner store. His eyes sparkled.

Now, before you miss the point, let me be clear: The point is *not* that if we give a little to God, he'll give a lot more back to us. That's garbage. I don't have time to go into everything the Bible has to say about financial principles. It certainly does teach that when we use money God's way, then, generally speaking, things will go better for us. There are notable exceptions, though. And all of that misses the point I'm trying to make.

In the middle school world, brightly colored rubber bands are really significant. But wait until the next hot thing comes along, and they're old news. When my students are grown and they find an old Silly Bandz in the back of a drawer, they will chuckle at how those things used to matter to them. When I gave that kid a dollar, I gave him real riches, from the world's perspective. Once the dollar appeared, it broke the illusion that those Silly Bandz mattered. Suddenly they seemed, well, silly. You can buy lots of Silly Bandz with a dollar. Or a soda. Or candy. They had been so conflicted about whether to give me one until they saw that dollar. Suddenly a half-dozen little hands produced a half-dozen Silly Bandz from secret stashes. After one glimpse of real riches, they were begging to trade.

But dollars are not real riches! This whole life is middle school, and how silly we must seem to the heavenly beings, down here trading, fighting, sweating, and cheating for Silly Bandz.

True riches. What could they be?

Our faith is so small. We actually believe the things of this world matter more than the things of the next world. We're so bedazzled by the Silly Bandz—by the beautiful beaches and delicious food and nice neighborhoods—we cannot even imagine true riches. No wonder Jesus was frustrated over and over again by the smallness of our faith.[10] I do not think our wrong notions about money come from valuing it too highly. I think we vastly underestimate God.

Do we really think that the One who thought up the beautiful places in this world will somehow fail to make heaven even better? When Jesus said there were many rooms in his Father's house, and that he was going to make a place for us, could it be that the One who created the entire cosmos might make something for us even better than what we can grab in this life?[11]

True riches. What could they be?

Let's just let our imagination run for a moment.

Imagine the Father entrusting faithful servant leaders with the rule of entire cities.[12] Or what if God wants to trust faithful architects with the power to design the laws of nature? What if God gave faithful musicians orchestras to conduct full of rustling leaves, flocks of birds, and angel songs. What if he gave artists a new color no one had ever seen before, or the power to create new colors, or the ability to paint things into reality. What epic goals soccer players will score when we can fly!

My wife is an actress in musical theatre. She is faithful to God, serving him and not her industry. I like to imagine Jesus introducing her to an audience of millions. "Ladies and gentlemen, may I have your attention. I want you to see what Lindsay can do. I made her, and I did a good job. So relax and enjoy the show!" So many long to perform, but in this world only a small fraction get to, and only people with money get to enjoy their gifts. I'd see shows all the time if I could afford it. In this world, only a fraction of those who would like to write get to publish. I understand how fortunate I am. But how many books would we need for all of us to read all the books we'd like to read over the course of forever? How many writers would get to publish then?

I'm using earthly things to glimpse things we cannot imagine. Real riches will be even more wonderful, even more exciting, and even more satisfying, not less. We fear that heaven will be boring because we lack faith in God's extravagant goodness and grace.

Jesus said, "Truly I tell you, at the renewal of all things, when the Son of Man sits on his glorious throne, you who have followed me will also sit on twelve thrones, judging the twelve tribes of Israel. And everyone who has left houses or brothers or sisters or father or mother or wife or children or fields for my sake will receive a hundred times as much and will inherit eternal life."[13]

Imagine the woman who always dreamed of being a mother but who remained childless because the right man never came along, and for God's sake she refused to marry the wrong man. Imagine this woman who never married, now in heaven, the mother of hundreds of former orphans who dreamed of having a mother.

The call to generosity is not a call to go without. Generosity is a call not to miss out.

"The kingdom of heaven is like treasure hidden in a field," Jesus said. "When a man found it, he hid it again, and then in his joy went and sold all he had and bought that field."[14]

In his *joy* he sold all he had.

We Can Only Dream

Lindsay and I are reevaluating how we use possessions in a fundamental way. The money we direct to God's purposes is the most significant thing we do with money, so it's a real joy for us to tithe to our church and support other things that matter. But this runs deeper than just designating a portion to God. That's a starting place, and if you haven't started there, I recommend it. But how we use the rest is just as important. Our dreams tend to be too small because our faith in God is too small. His dreams for us are bigger than we imagine.

For example, Lindsay and I have been dreaming about buying a retirement home somewhere peaceful. We live in an apartment in a noisy city perched atop ninety stairs we have to climb every time we come or go. We know at some point we'll be too old for this. Manhattan is so expensive we'll likely never own something here, so when we're no longer able to earn, it will become difficult to stay. After breathing the smog for a few decades, we dream about spending a season of our lives near the ocean. It's a good dream, and we might actually see it happen in this life.

It's a good dream, but it's a small dream. The other day we wondered to each other—what if we had different dreams? What if God's dreams were our dreams? For the money it would take us to purchase a retirement home, we could found an orphanage in many parts of the world. We could plant a church in some countries. Imagine that. We could make God's dreams come true. What could be more significant than that?

We're dreaming about starting a family, and family is good. Psalm 127 says, "Children are a gift from the Lord."[15] But I also know God is dreaming about families for all the orphans in the world. And we're starting to talk seriously about that. Imagine. We could make God's dreams come true. What could be more significant than that?

I'm a work in progress. I'm not writing to you as a person who successfully "died to self" and now lives only for God. I'm writing as a person whose ideas about significance have been rattled, and I'm trying honestly to sort this out along with you. Many of my own dreams are worthy of effort. They're good dreams. But they're like a candle in the sun of God's dreams. My dreams may or may not be worthy of this life God has given me. I am utterly certain God's dreams are.

From Scripture there are two things we can be sure of about the next life. We know God will be there. So whatever matters to God matters forever. Imagine what will happen in your heart when God welcomes you home.

We also know people will be there. God's Spirit is at work all over the world, drawing men and women and children to himself. He will succeed at saving people. Anything we do for people matters because people live forever. I pray you grasp this precious truth: If you use what you have for others, "you will be welcomed into eternal dwellings."[16]

I finished teaching in Harlem. Now I'm working to plant a church in Manhattan, and that's another kind of challenge altogether. Who knows what comes next? For now God is using my experience teaching in that school to shape my ministry in ways I never expected. Mostly, I've got a new notion about what matters. "How much better to get wisdom than gold, to get insight rather than silver!"[17] I actually understand that now. You could not pay me to give up what I've learned. Not for all the gold in the world would I trade it. Not now that I've had a taste of true riches.

One time I caught one of my students in a lie. His mother thanked me on the phone for staying after to give William extra help on Friday, and something didn't add up. I often did stay after, but had no plans to that Friday. I had an idea of what was happening. Earlier I overheard talk among the sixth-graders about going swimming after school on Friday. At the same time William would supposedly be getting extra help in math, girls his age would be in bikinis at a nearby pool. It didn't take a genius to figure out what was going on.

"Let me handle this, and I'll get back to you," I said.

I went and pulled him out of another class for a chat. Sixth-graders are always amazed to discover that you actually know stuff. When I said, "William, you're lying to your mother about Friday because you want to go see the girls in their bathing suits," he regarded me with the kind of anxious awe usually reserved for witch doctors and prophets. I continued, "There's nothing wrong with wanting to be with the girls. You are twelve. You should be willing to break federal law to be with the girls. But lying to your mother isn't cool. That's what I want to talk about."

His head dropped and his lip quivered. Huge, silent tears tumbled down his cheeks.

I softened and scooted my chair closer to put my arm around him. "Buddy, what's wrong? What's going on?"

He explained that ever since his father left, he and his mother didn't get along. They argued constantly. Listening to him sob and tell his story, my eyes welled up. I didn't care about my reputation.

"I'm so sorry. I have no idea what that feels like. My dad stuck with us. But you're gonna make it, man. You and your mom have to stick together. It's not going to be easy, but will you talk to her?"

This was not a flashy moment. There weren't any paparazzi snapping photos. No dramatic soundtrack filled the air. The scene did not close with a tidy fade-to-black. I let him stop in the rest room to wash his face and took him back to class. Later on, I called his mother and explained the situation and tried to help her think through how to start talking to William about his father and the changes their family had gone through.

This was not a flashy moment, but reader, it was *significant*. We can all name teachers who were important to us growing up. Do you think that kid is ever going to forget the day Mr. Travis cried with him?

A few months into my first year after leaving teaching, I began to miss my students. I made it through September and October, but then I just had to go back. I worked it out with my former principal to come back and do some tutoring each week. Forty hours a week with them might have been a little too much of a good thing, but absence makes the heart grow fonder, right?

I had no idea.

When I walked into the cafeteria—I'm going to treasure this moment forever—about fifty kids jumped up and rushed over, surrounding me, screaming and hugging. Some of the girls were crying. They were actually crying to see me. The boys were hugging me and giving me high fives and punching me. Their smiling faces . . . it was overwhelming.

I heard one of the boys say, "You'd'a thought Jay-Z come up in here!"

I suppose in the same way I'd forgotten or forgiven all the nastiness they sometimes dished out, they had forgotten or forgiven all the times I called home and got them in trouble, chewed them out, pressured them, kept them after school, or piled on the homework.

No one can ever take that away from me. It's mine forever. I might never do another thing the world regards as significant. But that moment is mine to keep and cherish for the rest of my days.

You know what that is? It is real treasure. What a wealthy man I am.

True riches. What could they be?

I think I have an idea.

Epilogue

In Christ, You Are Significant

It Comes at a Cost

I'm on to the next thing. My wife and I live in a part of Manhattan called Inwood. Many New Yorkers aren't even aware it exists. In many cities, "uptown" is where the rich people live. Here, it's the opposite. On a clear day from one of the rooftops in Inwood, you can only just make out the silhouette of the Empire State Building or the Chrysler Building. Many of the residents in our neighborhood travel downtown to bus tables or sling trash bags into trucks. To get to Inwood, you have to ride the A Train north, all the way to the end of the line, or the 1 Train so far uptown it climbs out of the tunnels and onto an elevated track, rattling the windows of grungy little bodegas and whipping the laundry strung between fire escapes into a flutter as it rumbles past. You have to pass through Harlem and then Washington Heights before you land in our little corner of the biggest city in America.

New York City is a thrilling place to live because of the wild diversity and opportunity to experience culture. Inwood residents form an eclectic mix of artists and professionals, firefighters and teachers, immigrants and the working poor. Most residents are Spanish—Inwood is sort of the "little Dominica" of New York City. From the view of the fancy condos perched alongside the Hudson River, you can see the towers of the Dyckman Housing projects just a mile to the west. On our floor we know a Dominican family and a young woman from France. An elderly couple from Japan lives in the apartment below ours.

The diversity and culture are wonderful, but they come at a cost. Our overpriced two-bedroom apartment is on the fifth floor. Lindsay and I lug groceries and laundry up and down ninety steps from the street. Sometimes I help the Japanese gentleman up the stairs to his apartment on the fourth floor. He's in his eighties and walks with a cane. I stand behind him to make sure he doesn't tumble backwards, put my hands on his back, and push him up each flight. In the summer months, we're both sweating from the effort by the time we reach the top. I don't speak any Japanese, and all he knows how to say in English is "Thank you."

My wife and I and a small band of others felt a calling to start a new church in our neighborhood, and so began Everyday Church.[1] We are a new spiritual family in the middle of it all. We are diverse in age, ethnicity, and income. Our tiny family is black, white, Asian, and Spanish. We are seniors, babies, middle-schoolers, and twenty-somethings. We have more single parents among us than couples, and more people who are exploring faith than who are certain about it. Everyone has a past and a story, and we really appreciate one another, believing that everyone has a future, too.

One of the things teaching in Harlem impressed upon me was the need for churches to come alongside schools and lend a hand. In situations where parents aren't willing or, more often, simply aren't able to be highly involved in schools, education suffers. PTAs on the Upper East Side can command "expected donations" of a thousand dollars per kid. Many of my students' parents worked multiple jobs just to keep them fed and clothed. Of course I can't help but care about students and education. Many others in our church do, as well, so we have donated school supplies, provided free tutoring, painted a huge mural at a public school, and will do whatever else we can to serve.

The trick has been to serve with no ulterior motives whatsoever. Our Lord is a foot washer, not a controller. If the schools ask for supplies, we do that. If they need math tutoring, we provide that. When and if anyone is interested in church or Jesus, they know how to find us. The beautiful irony of serving this way is that people are genuinely interested in who we are and why we do what we do. In my opinion, they are asking us to give the reason for the hope that we have.[2]

My experience in Harlem changed the way I do ministry in a broader sense, too. I no longer get as excited about the flash and glitz. It's those tiny moments when I notice God at work that get me out of bed each day—when a prayer is answered, when someone understands grace for the first time, when someone is genuinely excited to explore the Bible for the first time. I find significance in the stories of everyday people. These days, the only thing that excites me about a crowd is the people in it.

We End Where We Began

What could be *less* significant than a new church trying to take root and sprout in a city of millions and millions of people who aren't a part of a church? We don't wield a big budget or a constituency large enough to change laws. We're at the mercy of forces more powerful than we are. As I write this, NYC public schools just made a disappointing decision to forbid churches from renting school buildings for worship. If this decision holds, Everyday Church will be looking for a new place to gather, along with dozens of other churches in the city. We meet in a public school because we served them so much they invited us to. They actually want us to meet there. It'll be a lose-lose if we no longer can.

But God is bigger than all that, and he will have his way. I'm not concerned about us. I'm mostly concerned now about whether Christian people will represent Jesus well as this battle gains momentum. Will we harden our faces and our voices and demand our "rights"? Or will we be patient and gracious and love our neighbors well? Speaking for Everyday Church, I'll say this: We will continue to serve the students, teachers, and parents of our public schools cheerfully and wholeheartedly, regardless of whether we can gather in their buildings.

Nothing can stop love. The worst the world can muster against love is death. But when we nailed Love to the cross, we fulfilled Christ's mission to forgive. Where, death, is your victory? Reader, what could ever separate us from God's love? Love never fails.[3]

Sometimes my wife and I daydream about the houses we could afford for half of what we pay in rent. I'm not a glutton for punishment. Neither was Jesus, by the way. It was for the *joy* set before him that he endured the cross.[4] I've had a taste of what matters, and I can't get enough. When our little church gathered after hours in a local restaurant to witness our first baptism, it was so . . . significant. Struggling for the right words to explain the decision she'd made, a young Dominican woman performed an interpretive dance to a beautiful Spanish song about coming home. When my friend Larry lifted her out of the water and into her new life, you would have thought there were a thousand people in the room, we cheered so loudly.

What could be more significant than a new church trying to take root and sprout in a city of millions and millions of people who aren't a part of a church? And so we end where we began, with a true paradox: Helping to start a new church is one of the most insignificant things I can do. It is also the most significant.

This Wonderful Glimpse

Reader, you matter in the surprising way God is changing the world. I don't know how much of that truth you will get to see with your own eyes. God gave me a wonderful glimpse. Perhaps your faith is stronger than mine, and he knows you don't need it.

But it's coming. True riches and things that matter are coming. The God Who Matters is coming. You and I may never meet in this life, but one day, after all the days, when time slips away into ages of joy, we will meet. We'll welcome each other into our eternal dwellings like old friends and laugh about the Silly Bandz.

Friend, until then, please remember: In Christ, you are significant.

Discussion Questions

Chapter 1: About the Author

1. Who was your favorite teacher growing up? Why?
2. Have you ever had a cross-cultural experience? What was it like?
3. Can you think of some examples of things that seem insignificant but are actually very important?
4. Have you ever failed at something? What happened? How did it feel?
5. What are you hoping to get out of reading this book?

Chapter 2: First Things Last

1. What aspect of creation convinces you most of a Creator? The mountains? Oceans? Cosmos? Laughter? Music? People? Explain your response.
2. Why do you think God created the world?

3. Do you think the world is better than it used to be, or worse?

4. Have you ever had an experience when you knew God wanted you to do something specific? How did you know? What did you do?

5. How do you think God is currently trying to grow you?

Chapter 3: What Does He Want From Us?

1. Can you remember a time when you disobeyed your parents? What did you do? What happened?

2. What are some of the reasons people struggle to trust God?

3. Which sounds most difficult for you: loving God with all of your heart, all of your soul, or all of your mind? Which sounds easiest?

4. Is it easy or difficult for you to believe God loves you? Why?

5. Is Jesus enough for you?

Chapter 4: This is Personal

1. Describe your "daily grind." What fills most of your time?

2. Do you think it's possible to love others too much? Explain.

3. Have you ever sacrificed for another? What happened? How did they respond?

4. Have you ever drawn a boundary with someone? What happened? How did they respond?

5. Who in your life can you count on to give you godly advice about when to sacrificially love others and when to love and care for yourself?

Chapter 5: Insignificant

1. If a genie granted you three wishes, what would you wish for? Be honest.
2. What do you think Jesus meant when he said, "Unless you change and become like little children, you will never enter the kingdom of heaven" (Matthew 18:1–4)?
3. How do you think the disciples felt as Jesus washed their feet?
4. Have you ever "endured hardship as discipline"? Did that experience produce any "righteousness and peace" in you (Hebrews 12:7–11)?
5. Think about your life. Who will you serve as Jesus did? How? Be specific.

Chapter 6: What Only God Can Do

1. Have you ever experienced a clear answer to prayer? How did God come through?
2. Do you think prayer is difficult, easy, or both? In what ways?
3. When you read "The Lord's Prayer," what jumps out to you? How is Jesus' instruction about prayer unique?
4. What sorts of things do you face in your daily life for which you need God's power to do well, or to do right?

5. Who is your "our, we, us"? Who do you include in your prayers? Going forward, is there anyone else you intend to include?

Chapter 7: What Only You Can Do

1. Do you have any hidden talents or skills?
2. What has God entrusted to you? Make a list. Think about your time, talents, experiences, skills, possessions, relationships, education, and dreams.
3. Why do you think we're tempted to invest so much in things that do not ultimately matter?
4. In what ways are you currently investing in God's kingdom? In what ways do you hope to?
5. If you could accomplish just one thing with the rest of your life, what one thing would you do? Be realistic.

Chapter 8: Whatever You Do

1. What was your first job? Describe it.
2. What sorts of things do people work for? For what reasons do people work?
3. What difference do you think it would make in your life if you maintained an awareness that "It is the Lord Christ you are serving" (Colossians 3:24)?
4. What would it look like for you to "be a minister" in your neighborhood or family, at your job or school?
5. What one thing could you change to do "whatever you do" for God? Be specific.

Chapter 9: Welcome Forever

1. If your home caught fire and, as you fled, you had time to grab only three possessions, which would you take? Why?

2. Is it ever "right" to do "wrong"? Explain your response with an example.

3. Fill in the blank: "For heaven to be heaven for me, it will have to have _____." Why?

4. Who are you looking forward to reconnecting with in the next life?

5. What do you think God would like to accomplish *in* you during your lifetime? What do you think God would like to accomplish *through* you during your lifetime? Be specific.

Epilogue

1. Have your views of significance changed? How?

2. How will you change in response to your views?

Notes

Chapter 1: About the Author

1. "School from Hell," *New York Post,* June 26, 2011, www.nypost.com/p/news/local/manhattan/the_school_from_hell_nVS0ubg9F7uzULCHOrNh2H#ixzz1WYnMKy6H.
2. Matthew 7:7

Chapter 2: First Things Last

1. For more information about the New York City Teaching Fellows, visit www.nyctf.org.
2. 1 John 4:8
3. Genesis 6:5–6 NLT
4. Matthew 13:30
5. Genocide Intervention, accessed November 11, 2011, www.genocideintervention.net/.
6. 1 Samuel 15:23 NLT
7. Isaiah 64:6
8. Isaiah 53:2 NLT
9. Luke 22:64 NLT
10. Luke 23:34
11. 2 Peter 3:9 NLT
12. Nomi Network, accessed December 15, 2010, www.nominetwork.org/story.php#text. Please support Nomi Network!
13. NBC San Diego, accessed December 15, 2010, www.nbcsandiego.com/around-town/events/Nomi_Network_Named_Small_Charity_of_the_Year_San_Diego-106898148.html.

Chapter 3: What Does He Want From Us?

1. John 12:13
2. Mark 11:17
3. Matthew 22:29
4. Matthew 22:33
5. Matthew 22:36
6. Matthew 22:37–38
7. John 4:23–24
8. Matthew 11:30
9. Luke 12:48
10. 1 John 4:19
11. John 21:15–17

Chapter 4: This Is Personal

1. 1 John 3:18
2. For examples of people who weren't interested in following Jesus, see Mark 10:22 and John 6:66.
3. John 14:23
4. 1 John 2:5
5. Matthew 22:37–38
6. Matthew 22:39–40
7. According to one of the most widely recognized lists, composed by Rabbi Moshe ben Maimon, one of the greatest medieval Jewish scholars. Judaism 101, accessed November 11, 2011, www.jewfaq.org/613.htm.
8. Matthew 22:39
9. Matthew 11:19
10. Mark 1:35
11. For examples of how the New Testament uses the word *church*, see Colossians 1:24 and 4:15.
12. John 15:10, 12
13. 1 John 4:20
14. Isaiah 42:3
15. Revelation 5:11
16. Matthew 25:34–36
17. Matthew 25:37–39
18. Matthew 25:41–43
19. Matthew 25:44
20. Matthew 25:40
21. Matthew 25:45
22. Matthew 25:46
23. Matthew 18:6; Mark 9:42; Luke 17:2
24. 1 John 3:16
25. Romans 12:1

Chapter 5: Insignificant

1. John 13:3
2. John 13:3–5

3. Mark 3:17
4. Luke 9:54
5. Acts 12:2
6. Matthew 21:31
7. Matthew 18:1–4
8. Hebrews 12:7–11
9. 2 Corinthians 12:9
10. Luke 23:34
11. Luke 23:35
12. John 13:17

Chapter 6: What Only God Can Do

1. Matthew 6:7–8
2. Luke 11:1
3. Matthew 6:9–13
4. See Isaiah 65:24 and Mathew 6:8
5. See Luke 11:5–8 and 18:1–8. For a mysterious and thrilling glimpse into some of what goes on in the heavenly realm when we pray, see Daniel 10.

Chapter 7: What Only You Can Do

1. Romans 8:28
2. Romans 12:6
3. Matthew 25:14–18
4. Matthew 25:19–23
5. John 20:27
6. Matthew 25:24–30
7. Luke 19:22
8. Matthew 25:29
9. 1 Corinthians 12:7
10. Ephesians 2:10
11. 2 Chronicles 16:9
12. Philippians 2:13

Chapter 8: Whatever You Do

1. Matthew 7:12; Luke 6:31
2. I owe this perfect way to close a lesson, along with the idea for my two classroom rules and about a thousand other things, to my colleague and friend, Ms. May. She is a true master of the craft of teaching and a strong believer.
3. Colossians 3:23–24
4. Colossians 3:24
5. Matthew 13:54–55
6. Acts 4:13
7. Acts 18:3
8. 1 Peter 2:9
9. Exodus 31:1–11
10. Psalm 127:2

11. Luke 17:33 NLT
12. Learn more about NYC Salt at www.nycsalt.org.
13. God's Love We Deliver, https://www.glwd.org/press/kit.jsp, accessed October 19, 2011.
14. Aaron Brockett in a message, "Job Placement," May 15, 2011, www.tpcc.org/series/take-this-job-and-love-it/, accessed October 19, 2011.
15. I heard Greg Nettle share this challenge in a message called "Innumerable" on July 6, 2010, at the North American Christian Convention.
16. Ecclesiastes 12:12

Chapter 9: Welcome Forever

1. Luke 11:5–8
2. Luke 18:1–8
3. Matthew 21:31
4. Luke 16:8
5. Luke 16:9
6. Luke 16:10–13
7. Luke 16:14–15
8. 1 Timothy 6:10
9. Luke 16:11
10. For examples, see Matthew 14:31 and 16:8.
11. John 14:1–3
12. Luke 19:17
13. Matthew 19:28–29
14. Matthew 13:44
15. Psalm 127:3 NLT
16. Luke 16:9
17. Proverbs 16:16

Epilogue: In Christ, You Are Significant

1. www.everydaycc.com
2. 1 Peter 3:15
3. 1 Corinthians 15:55; Romans 8:35; 1 Corinthians 13:8
4. Hebrews 12:2